The Making of a Miracle

The Making of a Miracle

✦

A Couple's Journey in Faith

Bob & Joanne Wetzel

iUniverse, Inc.

New York Lincoln Shanghai

The Making of a Miracle
A Couple's Journey in Faith

iUniverse books may be ordered through booksellers or by contacting:

iUniverse
2021 Pine Lake Road, Suite 100
Lincoln, NE 68512
www.iuniverse.com
1-800-Authors (1-800-288-4677)

Wherever real names and identities have been used in this book, permission has been granted. Permission has also been granted for use with excerpts from previously published material.

ISBN-13: 978-0-595-36184-7 (pbk)
ISBN-13: 978-0-595-80631-7 (ebk)
ISBN-10: 0-595-36184-6 (pbk)
ISBN-10: 0-595-80631-7 (ebk)

Printed in the United States of America

Dedicated to...

all those who persevere
in praying and believing
that God can do what He
says He can.

FOREWORD

This story is about our journey in faith, the power of prayer and the faithfulness and goodness of our God. It is not our intent to be a theologically correct argument on the subject of miracles, it's simply a sharing of what we experienced and believe. We know what he did for us he wants to do for you, and pray our story will be an encouragement to you.

Some of it may sound familiar to many who were part of it, and to those who heard us speak of it, for we haven't been quiet about the great things God has done in our lives. We never want to forget. And so we have written it down—for ourselves, you, and those who haven't heard it at all. How else could we continue to give God glory and bear witness to the power of positive prayer and the unfathomable power released by community prayer?

> *"I kneel in prayer to the Father. All beings in heaven and on earth receive their life from him. God is wonderful and glorious. I pray that his Spirit will make you become strong followers and that Christ will live in your hearts because of your faith. Stand firm and deeply rooted in his love. I pray that you and all of God's people will understand what is called wide and long or high and deep. I want you to know all about Christ's love, although it is too wonderful to be measured. Then your lives will be filled with all that God is.*
>
> *I pray that Christ Jesus and the church will forever bring praise to God. His power at work in us can do far more than we dare ask or imagine."*
> *Amen.*

—Ephesians 3:14-21

1

"Let everything that has breath praise the Lord. Praise the Lord."

—*Psalm 150*

We begin the journey in Boynton Beach, Florida, February 2003. Joanne and I had planned a reunion for some friends and relatives, almost all of whom went to the same elementary school in Queens, New York, many years before. All in all about 25 people. The party was held in our condominium's club house and was a great success. When it was over, I started loading the car to bring everything back to our condo, but I had to keep stopping to rest. After one or two trips I couldn't continue at all; my easy, natural rhythm of breathing seemed to have been sucked out of me and with it, any strength I had. A friend who was helping me ended up doing the whole thing. Joanne asked, more surprised than concerned, "what's the matter with you, why are you sitting and letting Joey do it all?" I told her I just couldn't do it, "I can't catch my breath". This was the first time such profound symptoms appeared.

When we returned to New York, and I saw my pulmonalogist, he noticed I was coughing a lot in the waiting room and that walking the short distance from the waiting room to the examination room caused me to be out of breath. After checking me and running some tests, he said something about my lungs not supplying enough oxygen and thought a Cat Scan might tell us what was cauing these symptoms.

◆　　◆　　◆

The doctor told us that the Cat Scan idicated Idiopathic Pulmonary Fibrosis (IPF), a lung disease we had never heard of before. As he went on to explain that it was progressive and fatal, his words caused a sharp pain in my heart and seeds of fear were deeply planted there. The only way to rule IPF out or confirm it was through a lung biopsy. Because Bob's lungs were already fragile (due to lung surgery he had six years earlier) he had to have an open lung biopsy.

◆　　◆　　◆

Neither Joanne nor I are worriers—things easily roll off our backs, and especially with health issues, we generally have positive, "everything-will-be-fine" attitudes. My response to "What did the doctor say? Usually was, "He didn't say I'm gonna die" meaning anything short of that wasn't worth worrying or talking about. This time was different. He did say it. I can remember a deep stillness coming over me. Perhaps shock, perhaps denial. I don't really know. I could hear Joanne talking to the doctor as if from a distance. She asked a lot of questions and although I felt somewhat out of it, I knew she wasn't getting the answers she wanted. Even then, I don't believe either of us truly expected that scary diagnosis would be confirmed, and we certainly had no idea how fast and how bad it would get.

We told our family and a few close friends about what was going on and asked them to pray for me. Two of those friends were directing our parish Passion Play which we had founded 24 years earlier. The play was presented as a Lenten Prayer and each practice began by circling up and praying in community. Bernadette and Paul asked if we wanted that community to know of our situation and we replied, yes of course, we need their prayers.

Father Smith, one of our parish priests, immediately offered to come to our house and anoint me—administer the Sacrament of the Sick. He said he could do it privately or with some friends, quickly adding, "Oh, maybe you don't want people to know." Again our reply—we want everyone to know so they'll pray for us. After Father anointed me, he invited everyone to come up one at a time and lay hands on me and Joanne and pray over us. What a blessed man I was, receiving a healing sacrament and having friends who were happy to pray over me. "…surely the presence of the Lord was in this place…" This was the first of many times we were lifted up by community prayer.

In order to more easily reach many people, Joanne sent emails to some friends and family, and asked our good friend Richie to forward them to our church community. It seems we were always asking someone to pray for us and with us. It became our mantra and eventually our life saver.

And so the computer became an integral part of my healing process. It was the glue that kept all of us together in prayer. While phone calls may have done the job, I don't believe it would have been as effective in bringing us together at the same time and keeping us of the same mind.

As we experienced our hopes and fears, many stood by us. They knew when we were up and when we were down—when we had absolute trust in God and when we were wavering. Technology made so many part of us, part of our experience, it helped us walk a closer walk.

When Joanne wrote, letting them know what was happening and requesting constant prayers, they responded by becoming a band of prayer warriors storming the gates of heaven. I'm reminded of a story in scripture, Luke 18:1-8, where Jesus uses a parable to show the need for constant prayer. "There was a judge, a godless man who had contempt for everyone. A widow came to him frequently to appeal to him for justice against a man who had harmed her. The judge ignored her for awhile, but eventually she got on his nerves. I fear neither God or man but this woman bothers me. I'm going to see she gets justice for she is wearing me down with her constant coming."

Then the Lord said "If even an evil judge can be worn down, don't you think that God will surely give justice to his people who plead with Him day and night."
We were that widow constantly asking through prayer for a healing.

◆   ◆   ◆

1st email

Subject: Prayer Request
Date: 4/21/2003   7:41 p.m.

It's the Easter Season—new life is everywhere—even in technology! Our computer died some time in January (we never did receive those emails you may have sent) but now we're up and running with a new address. Just in time to let you know we need your prayers.

Bobby's been having difficulty breathing, has had a Cat Scan and is having a lung biopsy Friday, April 25ᵗʰ @ 9 a.m. We know God hears and answers the prayers of righteous men and women, and so we ask you to please join with our family in praying for a full and total healing—we pray that God will replace his scarred, diseased lungs with new lungs, in Jesus' name.

We're believing and trusting in God's love, mercy and faithfulness. (When or if we've prayed together, you've heard me say: "When the praises go up, the healings come down")—Praise God!

Love,
Joanne

2

"As they prayed, the place where they gathered shook, and they were filled with the holy spirit."

—*Acts 4:31*

The biopsy confirmed the initial diagnosis. Bobby had IPF—it was inoperable, there was no cure, no proven therapy and life expectancy was two to possibly six years. On receiving that firm diagnosis, the seeds of fear planted after the Cat Scan exploded into profound sadness. And that deep-rooted sadness never left me. It was my core feeling either on or just under the surface, for the months to come. I remember trying not to think about what the doctor was saying or all the tremendously discouraging information I had learned about the disease since the Cat Scan. I forced myself to believe this was going to be different. Bobby was strong and breathing pretty good for the most part. He'd just take it easy, eat healthy, get lots of rest and we'd do whatever was necessary to beat this.

As much as we could, we clung to our natural positiveness. Bobby was doing better emotionally than I was. By Sunday evening in the hospital, visitors gone, I began to fall apart. I laid on the bed next to Bobby, scared and brokenhearted. Always before, having his arms around me and hearing his reassuring words calmed me; not that night, the fear and tears wouldn't stop. God help us, I kept thinking, help me pull myself together. I hated that I might be bringing Bobby down with me, so I sat up, still heavy hearted and said, "Let's pray". We opened a prayer book to the reading for that day, entitled: "Glimpsing the Lord Energizes Us".

Excerpts from <u>Living Faith,</u> Daily Catholic Devotions—April 27th, 2004

"When fear grips us, when we convince ourselves the worst is going to happen, when we see only dead ends and limited options, then we allow ourselves to become disempowered. Instead of remembering that with God all things are possible, we move into panic, self-pity or even despair. With no sense of direction, we distance ourselves from those we love most or from those activities which give meaning to life. Enthusiasm and energy drain away as we become preoccupied with our problems; depression sets in as we focus only on our losses—or potential losses. In effect, we become the living dead—until, that is, we catch a glimpse of the Lord who has been standing in our midst all along. Then, recognizing his face, we know peace and joy once more." E.A. Stewart

WOW—we knew God had led us to this reading which spoke powerfully to our hearts. We felt his peace and his presence. If we could take his hand, day by day, we'd be okay. He'd see us safely through.
The next day's <u>Living Faith</u> reading continued to support and comfort us;

Excerpts from Shaking the Ground of Our Hearts, Monday, April 28th

As they prayed, the place where they gathered shook, and they were filled with the holy Spirit…Acts 4:31 "…the power referred to in the Acts of the Apostles is shaking the ground of our hearts…It is the overwhelming power of the presence of the Spirit of Jesus. May the place in my life from which I pray shake the power of God that breaks upon me." Sr. K. J. Hermes, F.S.

And as we prayed, the spirit broke upon us as well, banishing fear and kindling a deeper belief in the overwhelming power of prayer.

◆   ◆   ◆

2nd email

Subject: He gives wonderful comrades to us...
Date: 5/1/2003 6:20 p.m.

Bob is finally home from the hospital and beginning treatment for pulmonary fibrosis. Monday we meet with the doctor and get the results of the pathology reports and a course of action. We're holding all positive thoughts and expecting a full recovery because our God is a faithful God and we ask in Jesus' name.
"Whatever you ask for in prayer, believe that you have received it, and it will be yours." Mark 11:24.
We're believing (most of the time). Your prayers and all the love you pour on us (visits, cards, calls, masses, etc.) are a tremendous support—we couldn't get through this time without you.
We're not letting you off the hook, keep those prayers coming! Thanks for everything.

We love you,
Joanne & Bobby

◆   ◆   ◆

Now the miracle begins to unfold…

3

"Dear woman, why do you involve me? Jesus replied. 'My time has not yet come.' This, the first of his miraculous signs, Jesus performed at Cana in Galilee. He thus revealed his glory, and his disciples put their faith in him."

—*John 2:4, 11*

Joanne was never content with one doctor's opinion and wanted another one from a Manhattan doctor, preferably from Columbia Presbyterian Hospital, but had no idea who to call. She asked our neighbor, a nurse, if she knew of anyone. Diane remembered our best friend's son was a doctor and suggested we ask him. He's not a pulmonalogist and not in NY, but he did some quick research and got back to us with the name and phone number of whom he was told was the best pulmonary specialist in the city—Dr. Arcasoy at Columbia P. H. Joanne felt an immediate surge of hope—sure that this was where God was leading us. When she called for an appointment however, the receptionist wouldn't give her one, advising that Dr. Arcasoy only does transplants and only on a doctor's referral. It seemed like she kept trying to get Joanne off the phone, but Joanne wouldn't hang up. Finally Joanne said to the receptionist, "Look we've been praying that we could get an appointment..." "You what?" Silence, then, "Hold on." Then a male voice came over the phone. Joanne explained the situation and he said "We only do transplants, but there's a doctor who runs a clinic here specializing in IPF, Dr. Paul Simonelli." He took our phone number and said he'd call Dr. Simonelli and give it to him . He also gave us the Doctor's number so that if we didn't hear from him by the next afternoon, we could call. Joanne thanked him and asked to whom was she talking. He replied, "Dr. Joshua Sonett"…the surgeon who eventually performed my lung transplant.

◆   ◆   ◆

3rd email

Subject: We're walking by Faith
Date: 5/6/03   11:30 p.m.

Pathology reports confirm Bob has idiopathic pulmonary fibrosis (scarring of the lung tissue) and emphysema. That's the bad news.
The good news is it's in the early stages and Prednisone (he's taking) is considered to be a miracle drug. And, most importantly, GOD IS WITH US THROUGH YOUR LOVE AND PRAYERS IN A VERY POWERFUL WAY! We want to try to share a few of the many signs He gives us, small and big because you help us recognize them:
-Getting great parking spaces wherever we go.
-Having a really rough day, moving towards despair, when grace causes me to open my <u>Living Faith</u> devotional to where we read, "Do not allow fear to disempower you, but remember that with God all things are possible." The perfect reading, at the perfect time—He does not abandon us!
-Getting an apt. with a top doctor at Columbia Presbyterian for a 2nd opinion (Tues., May 13th, 11:30 a.m.)—when they only take doctor referrals & only for lung transplants; but I was persistant and said: "we're praying you'll see us for a 2nd opinion", "You're what?" and then one of the lung surgeons got on the phone and as we talked I menitoned Bob's lung surgeon, and it "just so happened" that he not only knew him, but he's his partner!

-Attending a Healing Mass in Dobbs Ferry, not knowing anyone and seeing the names of old friends on a welcome brochure.

-Fr. Tom McDonald celebrating the Mass—I don't think we'd seen him since he left St. Peters. (When we were in St. Peter's a very short time, it was Fr. Tom who allowed us to bring in the Passion Play, the Genesis 2 Adult and High School Programs and others—he barely knew us but when we asked, he said yes and we, and our faith community, were blessed).

-Having the music ministry playing and singing "How Great is Our God" just as we were being prayed over, one of our very favorites—"….He said He'd never leave us, put your faith in Me…" And we do.

-Last but not least, YOU are a beautiful sign of God's love and faithfulness. Thank you.

And thanks too for daily lifting Bobby up to God, asking and expecting Him to replace the diseased lungs with new, healthy ones, in the precious name of Jesus. Through your love and prayers we are able to stand strong in faith trusting in God's mercy, His everlasting love and faithfulness.

We wish you (at least) all the love, peace and joy we have been blessed with,

Love you all,
Joanne & Bob

◆   ◆   ◆

After my diagnosis, I had a lot of time to think. The disease was progressive and incurable, and I wondered why I seemed to be handling it so well. Am I denying that this was really happening to me? Many times Elizabeth Kubler-Ross' stages of dying came to mind. She had worked with terminally ill patients and had hypothesized that there were five stages that the terminally ill usually go through. They all seemed reasonable to me.

Denial—No, it's not happening to me. The report must have gotten mixed up.

Anger—Why is it happening to me? Mad at God or the world.

Bargaining—Bargaining with God. If you let me live, I'll do this or that.

Depression—Withdrawal from life, family and friends.

Acceptance—It's OK, I'm ready. Fear or worry not really present.

I never got angry or mad or wondered why me? The idea that I was singled out for the disease never crossed my mind. My cardiologist, when visiting me in the hospital right after the diagnosis, put it very succinctly, "You were dealt a hand, now you have to live with it". Stuff happens, and it rains on the just and the unjust comes to mind.

I never tried to make deals with God for a healing. I prayed for one but never a quid pro quo.

Depression never seemed to rear it's ugly head either, unless finding it a little harder to laugh at things was depression.

This leaves acceptance and I had trouble believing that I could get there without going through the first four stages. It didn't seem logical, so I continually came back to denial and wondered if I was stuck there. I would like to say that I was positive that God would heal me and therefore, none of these stages applied, but I can't because I wasn't sure. Sometimes it was difficult to walk by faith and not by sight; I didn't want to die, but I wasn't afraid either. When I thought about it, my only concern was the pain and loneliness my sweetheart would experience.

4

"Jesus said, 'I tell you that if two of you on earth agree about anything you ask for, it will be done for you by my Father in heaven.'
For where two or three come together in my name, there I am
with them."

—Matthew 18:19-20

4th email

Subject: Feelin' Good (God)
Date: 5/13/2003   6:19 p.m.

Hi Guys,

*Went to Columbia Presbyterian Hospital today, saw Dr. Paul Simonelli.
He was extremely thorough in examining Daddy and the many reports, x-
rays, Cat-Scans, etc. we brought with us dating back to 1995; also in inter-
viewing us. Because we believe God arranged this appointment, we felt we
were where we were meant to be and feel good about his diagnosis, which in
itself doesn't sound very promising. (Walking by faith and truth—nothing's
impossible with God.)*

*Daddy has a "classic" case of Idiopathic Pulmonary Fibrosis—had it way
back in 1996, possibly even 1995(earliest x-ray). The good thing about
that is it's obviously very slow moving. The other good thing is that the doc-*

tor (as many before him) said that Daddy appears to be in a lot better condition than the "numbers" indicate. He's doing very well (God again).

The doctor does not believe Prednisone is the answer, wants him off it almost in accordance with our local pulmonoligist's schedule: 40 mg. 3 weeks, 20 mg. 2-3 weeks, 10 and then none. (Dr. S. had intended to keep him on 10 mg. possibly forever.)

Unfortunately, however, there really is no medication at this time to treat it. Interferon may be promising—some new tests being done on it. Tests done recently weren't handled correctly. (Article Aunt Tibby had sent from the NY Times.)

At this time he scheduled Daddy for a Pulmonary Stress Test (probably in June), and then we'll see him again after it. Will provide a prognosis and therapy after reviewing those test results along with all the info/reports/x-rays he looked at today.

Says exercise is the best thing you can do to get oxygen into the body—lungs are only a conduit. Talked about possibly getting into a Pulmonary Rehab Program. (Someone praying for Daddy told us last week that Helen Hayes Hospital has one, and we were looking into it and intended to ask the doctor if it might be beneficial). He also talked about the possibility of exercising with oxygen (I had read about that in "Alternatives" and it was one of the questions I was going to ask). See how God directs our paths when we lean on him! And that's where we are to date!

Dr. Simonelli will be working with our local doctor—says he didn't miss it, it's extremely difficult to diagnose. Simonelli said he's looking at the films in hindsight, already knowing what Daddy has, and looking only for that.

Also he said it's all he does—he should be able to see it. Same with prescribing Prednisone—it's what most pulmonary doctors do—it's right out of the book and appears to be "the" answer.

So here we are feeling very "lifted up" coming home singing "Thank you Jesus" and feeling assured as Daddy said confidently: "We're gonna beat this thing"—Amen!!! "...not on our faith alone, but on the faith of the church"—our church, all of us, all our family and friends praying—under the direction and everlasting love and mercy of God!

Love you so much,
Mom

◆   ◆   ◆

Well "our church" was not somewhere out there, it was very present to us. The support that began to pour in from family and friends was beyond heartwarming, and it never waned.

There were many Get Well cards, notes, Mass cards and phone calls with offers to do whatever we needed. They picked up groceries, dropped off meals and stopped by for short, impromptu visits.

I've lost track of how many Masses, novenas and rosaries were said on my behalf.
I even had two elementary schools praying for me, St. Peter's in Haverstraw, NY, and St. John's Academy in New Jersey.

The 4th grade at St. John's prayed for me daily by name. And one little 3rd grader who was experiencing serious separation anxiety was able to leave her Mom and go into her classroom by thinking of my struggle to walk and exercise, and praying for me.

Our pastor, Father Madden, and his associate, Father Smith, called and visited bringing the Eucharist, and words of understanding and encouragement. They didn't come alone, we knew they were praying for us and requesting prayers at their liturgies and the love and prayers of our fellow parishioners came with them. Through them we experienced "church" and our priests, in a richer and more beautiful way.

5

"Trust in him at all times O people; pour out your hearts to him for God is our refuge."

—Psalm 62:8

5th email

Subject:…in the palm of His hand.
Date: 5/21/2003   11:12 p.m.

Dear Family, Friends—Prayer Partners,

Just a quick update. Bobby had a Cardio-Pulmonary Stress Test this morning at Columbia Presbyterian hospital and did very well. The doctor there, Dr. Bartel, said his lung capacity while exercising was 70-80% of what someone without the disease would have. Further, he said he most likely has IPF 6-7 years and if it continued to move slowly, it could possibly be another 6-7 years before it got any worse. He will be forwarding the results to Dr. Simonelli (who requested and scheduled the test) and we will be meeting with him next Friday, May 30th. We expect he'll be putting Bobby on an exercise program at that time.

As we stepped out of the car on our return home, we stepped onto a big, bright rainbow on the wet ground. I guess that was just in case we didn't feel his presence in the positive test results and Dr. Bartel's encouraging words! Thanks be to God, who alone is worthy of all praise!

And thanks and love to all of you,
Joanne & Bobby

◆   ◆   ◆

We sought to surround ourselves with prayer, positive people and things that kept us strong in believing. Christian music met that criteria and filled our home with God-loving, faith-building praise and worship songs all day long. Our favorites were on America's 25 Favorite Praise and Worship Songs, Vol.2, which contained many songs we use to sing at the Amazing Grace Prayer Meetings in Howard Beach, NY. They built us up, reminding us that we were already victorious in Christ and had nothing to fear with our Mighty God in control.

Another aid I kept focused with was an optical illusion piece my brother and sister-in-law gave me. When looked at from one angle, it looked like a bunch of sticks, but from another angle, the name of JESUS appeared big and bold. Joanne placed it on a table across the room from where I sat during most of the day. Every time I picked up my head or glanced that way I was treated to the name of JESUS. I was reminded many times a day that He was my hope.

It was a good conversation piece as well. Visitors would wonder about "the sticks" and then move around the room trying to make something of it. Some took longer than others, but eventually everyone saw JESUS clearly. I know I saw him even more clearly too, through their caring visits.

◆   ◆   ◆

6th email

Subject: Pray without ceasing…
Date: 5/30/2003   2:16 p.m.

Hi Guys,

2nd visit with Dr. Simonelli (Columbia Presbyterian) this morning. Not feeling as "up" as we did after last week's meeting with Dr. Bartel, but still believing he's the doctor the Lord has guided us to.

Dr. Bartel had given us some positive numbers "if it [the disease] continued to move slowly"[it could be "possibly six to seven years before it got any worse"]. Dr. Simonelli said it's too soon to determine the rate of the disease's progression. He did say however that Daddy is currently in good condition, confirmed by his physical appearance, exam and mild symptoms of IPF, and also by the good results of the pulmonary stress test. We talked again about there being no currently available proven therapy for IPF, and then about Daddy getting into some possible upcoming trials of medications, and about interferon-gamma being a possibility—all in the future.

For now, Dr. Simonelli's recommending (and gave us a prescription for) a pulmonary rehabilitation program (at a hospital almost in our backyard. God is so good) which calls for exercising 2-3x a week for 14 weeks to max- imize breathing efficiency and getting the most oxygen into his system. He wants Daddy to continue tapering off Prednisone and gave us a plan for reducing the many other lung meds he's on which were prescribed before his being diagnosed with IPF. He still sees exercise and some weight loss as the way to go. Our next appointment is August 12th. Won't he be surprised when he sees the great strides Daddy will have made!

And so we remain where we are safest and feel most at home—in the hands and heart of God!
Continue to storm the gates of heaven with your prayers—they are being answered!

We love you,
Mom & Dad

It was during this appointment that Dr. Simonelli first mentioned lung transplant. It didn't seem significant at the time. It was in the context of an apology—as he talked about the lack of effective therapy for Bob's disease, he said how sorry he was that he couldn't offer him a lung transplant. We understood him to say that the cutoff date was 60 and Bob was 66. It had never entered my mind, Bobby's either. He responded in that manner: "not a problem, not looking for one." As we talked about it months later, we realized how naive we were then—so totally ignorant of how deadly and fast moving this disease was. Bobby was still feeling pretty good, still breathing on his own, and we were still believing it would be another several years before it got any worse.

Early in July we went, as usual, to the Pocono Mountains with our children and grandchildren on family vacation. But this was unlike our previous vacations; we didn't arrive lighthearted and anticipating a great time. This time we each came with Bobby's bleak diagnosis weighing heavily on our minds and hearts and hoping to find strength in unity.

It was hard to get into vacation mode at first, as we were forced to accept the grim reality of Daddy's failing health—he wasn't doing the shopping and planning any family meals or outings like he had before, instead he was taking a back seat and forced to conserve his energy, if he was going to be able to do any fun things with the family at all. Our kids were great; they pulled their positive outlooks and wonderful senses of humor to the forefront, determined to see that everyone enjoyed this time we had together.

Bobby and I awoke early each morning and while the rest of the family slept, we sat on the upstairs back porch alternating between soaking in the quiet beauty of the still countryside, sharing feelings and saying our prayers—the Psalms. It was our daughter-in-law Kathy who first came upon us and asked if she could join us. Before the week ended, all our children were up and taking turns reading the psalms and praying with us. Even our grandchildren, quietly coming and going, respected this special morning time. They didn't complain about breakfast being late, they waited and hopefully took some of it in.

No, this wasn't a usual family vacation. It was extraordinary—mornings filled with the peace of Christ, carried over into fun, laughter-filled days and nights…God's in his heaven, all's right with the world.

6

"Do not be anxious about anything, but in everything, by prayer and petition, with thanksgiving, present your requests to God. And the peace of God, which transcends all understanding, will guard your hearts and your minds in Christ Jesus."

—*Phillipians 4:6-7*

7th email

Subject: May His light shine in the darkness of our fears…
Date: 7/25/2003   1:43 p.m.

Dear Family, Friends—Prayers,

Just in case you've been taking a little prayer break for the summer, we're back to say we need your prayers now more than ever.

As of Tuesday, Bobby has to rely on supplemental oxygen—he doesn't need it at rest, but with walking/exertion he needs help. That development knocked the wind out of our sails and hope from our hearts. When we got up from our knees, we met with Dr. Simonelli (Columbia Presbyterian Hospital) who says it isn't necessarily an indication of drastic deterioration—the nature of the disease is that it sometimes ebbs and flows. We'll be seeing him again in a couple of weeks.

In the meantime we're trying to focus on the gift liquid oxygen is rather than the need for it. We're working at not allowing fear to disempower us but instead to remind us that nothing's impossible with God, and that the perfect love of Jesus casts out all fear. As I said, we're "working on it" and I guess (through the power of prayer) we're doing pretty good—so we know He's working in us.

While you're praying for a miracle for Bobby, pray for all those who don't believe and thank God that He made you to believe.

Enjoy these beautiful days of summer!

Love you all,
Joanne & Bobby

◆   ◆   ◆

When I could still leave the house with portable oxygen, Joanne and I would go to healing masses or services. Different friends would call up and let us know where they were being held, and Joe and Barbara often picked us up and brought us there.

My mind would sometimes wander during the service and I would think about God in relation to healing. Intellectually I knew that God could heal everyone there. He is all merciful and powerful, but in all probability He wouldn't. I wondered why, if there was to be a healing, He would pick me and not someone else. What criteria would He use? Was I more deserving than others? I didn't think so.

I'd look around the church and see young mothers with small children obviously going through chemo treatments waiting on line to be prayed over. Young adults, crippled or spastic were also waiting for their turn. I thought to myself, I'm sixty-six years old, I lived my life and how sad it would be for those young children to be without a mother, and how it would be "better" if she was the one who was healed. But I never got off the line. Those thoughts were noble, theoretical or hypothetical. What I was dealing with was personal and the reality was that I wanted to be healed. This happened the first few times I went to healing services. Eventually, those thoughts ceased coming to mind.

◆   ◆   ◆

One of the women who prayed over Bob at the first healing mass we attended, said God was sending angels with his healing and suggested that we go through our house, one room at a time with our bible in hand and pray scripture—we understood that she was telling us we needed to rebuke the devil and put on the armor of Christ, and we did.

That same week, in Florida, a favorite cousin attended a prayer meeting, one we regularly attended when we were there. He was prayed over for Bobby and was told to pray daily, without ceasing, for the angels were bringing Bobby's healing. We saw this as another confirmation of God's desire to heal Bobby.

We came away from our first healing Mass with renewed hope and with a prayer that we said our goodnights with each night. It continues to be a stronghold for us even today. It's from <u>Rise and Be Healed</u> *by Father Peter McCall and Mary Ann Lacey.*

"Let us pray:
Father, in Jesus' name, I acknowledge that no evil can come against me. May your light shine in the darkness of my fears. I believe that I am

under the power and authority of the Name of Jesus. Therefore, I am safe and free from all danger. I am sustained and supported with the help of Heaven itself. Angels have been assigned to watch over and protect me all the days of my life. I am reminded that the Perfect Love of Jesus casts out all fear. The Psalms tell me, "The Lord is my light and my salvation; whom should I fear? The Lord is my life's refuge; of whom should I be afraid? In confidence and with trust, I believe the Lord will give me the courage just when I need it. I take comfort in knowing that the Lord is my helper and protection. The Lord is my refuge and my fortress, my God in whom I trust. How great is your goodness, oh God. You are ever present to me. You have never abandoned me. You are always with me. I have nothing to fear for I place my trust in knowing that you are watching over me. I offer you my thanksgiving and praise and adoration all the days of my life. Amen."

While I was always aware of the reality that not everyone who prays gets what they ask for, Bobby and I always prayed expecting a healing. In making any plans now, we'd say: "we'll prepare for the worst and hope for the best". I brought that same philosophy to Bobby's healing as well. I'd acknowledge that God's ways are above our ways, and that my understanding is so limited, but that his love is limitless. So I hoped for the best, and God continually bolstered my faith with signs of his presence that pointed to a healing.

7

"If you remain in me and my word remains in you, ask whatever you wish, and it will be given to you. This is to my Father's glory, that you bear much fruit, showing yourselves to be my disciples."

—*John 15:7-8*

During this time, and from the very beginning, we prayed together daily, morning, noon and night asking God for a miracle and praising him for his goodness and faithfulness to us. Whenever it was a particularly tough day, and especially as Bobby's breathing got more difficult, and he needed more and more oxygen, we'd open up our Bible seeking comfort and direction from the Lord. His word never came back empty and always brought us to verses of encouragement and hope, instructing us also to persevere in prayer. He was hearing and answering.

And in obedience, our <u>Psalms for Today</u> and all our devotionals were daily companions and we prayed and prayed and prayed. Our favorite psalms were Psalm 23, The Lord is My Shepherd; Psalm 30, A Prayer of Thanksgiving; Psalm 66, A Song of Praise and Thanksgiving; Psalm 91, God our Protector. Psalm 116, 117 and 118, Someone Saved from Death Praises God; In Praise of the Lord, and A Prayer of Thanks for Victory. And so we prayed "without ceasing" sometimes with conviction, sometimes begging—always believing He was listening and was working to good in our lives—sometimes just hoping for, other times, truly expecting a miracle.

◆   ◆   ◆

Knowing we weren't praying alone was a great encouragement. People everywhere were praying for us and letting us know they were. We regularly received phone calls, cards and emails from our prayer communities in Rockland, Queens, Nassau and Suffolk counties in New York, and from extended communities in Florida, Tennessee, New Jersey, Pennsylvania and North Carolina who also had prayer warriors on my behalf.

Some good friends shared that God had put it on their hearts to pray for me throughout the day and night and I was always in their thoughts. Others sought out Charismatic prayer meetings and were prayed over on my behalf. While still others in small communities got together at regular intervals to pray in unison.

There were people who were moved to go back to church on Sundays and others who began going to daily mass and communion. Many were praying daily instead of occasionally, and in some instances prayer was becoming spontaneous instead of ritual or formal. From many of them we heard of changes in their spiritual life and a deepening relationship with God because of their prayer "marathons". All shared they were experiencing a renewal in their belief in the power of prayer and God's working in their lives. All in all, it seemed to us that the Spirit was moving mightily through my illness, and I was humbled and gratified to witness it.

Friends would drop by to pray over me, anointing me with holy water from Lourdes, Medjogorie, Fatima and Our Lady of the Snows in Illinois. I was anointed as well with Padre Pio blessed oil, St. Anne de

Beaupre oil and anointing oil used by a healing priest in his services. There were blessed prayer cloths too, and St. Jude and Mother Theresa relics—all intended to further empower our prayers and help gain the miracle we were seeking. We used them all with reverence and in good faith knowing that these sacramentals, in and of themselves alone, are powerless. We realize and believe that it is the faith in Jesus Christ that is important. We used these items as an expression of that faith and an aid to increase it.

We reverently and with expectation prayed with everything that anyone brought or sent us: water, oil, relics, rosary tapes, rosary beads, prayers, the Chaplet of Divine Mercy, etc. We called upon the Blessed Mother and every saint we ever felt any connection to, to intercede for us—especially St. Mother Theresa, St. Anne, St. Jude, Padre Pio, and Father Salonus Casey. So much so, that I can't be used to further someone's canonization because there was no one in particular that we asked to intercede for us. We called on the community of saints, particularly our family who knew and loved us. Our cries went up to Jesus Christ, Father God and the Holy Spirit. Praying always for the protection of the Precious Blood of Jesus, and safekeeping in His most Sacred Heart.

◆   ◆   ◆

As time passed and any remnants of Bobby's good health with it, our children visited more frequently and Laurie & Anthony, who live in Tennessee, were flying home as often as possible and staying longer each time. They couldn't do enough for us. Except for the deeply felt sadness over Bob's deteriorating health, there were many good times and beautiful family sharing experiences where praying together led to expressions of love, appreciation, admiration and other meaningful sentiments that lifted my sweetheart's spirit and enveloped him completely in love. There were moments like these continually through the months, not only with our children but with all of our family and friends, old and new. So many deeds and expressions of love poured out on us.

Bernadette "the faithful" as we came to refer to her, was a bottomless pit of love who daily walked the walk with us. Bernadette's one of those rare, beautiful people who feels deeply, loves generously and isn't afraid to get up close, grab your hand and hold you up. We knew Bernadette when she was a young girl in our Parish Passion Play. Now she brought her girls to cheer us up. She visited often and called every day, always leaving us with a smile and in better spirits than she found us.

◆   ◆   ◆

Our dear friend and next door neighbor was another daily companion. Not fully recovered from his own serious health problems, he managed to shower us with love. Joanne and I wonder if we would have been able to make it through without him. A day didn't go by that Tom didn't pop in for a visit. On good days we'd have coffee or maybe lunch and some light conversation. On bad days, he wouldn't stay, but would let us know he was right next door and available. And all days, he brought some normalcy and lots of encouragement. He was someone we could rely on, a bright spot in an otherwise dark day.

When I was no longer able to get to church, Tom with his wife Eileen (a Eucharistic minister), brought us the Eucharist after Mass every Sunday for six months. Tom would proclaim the Readings and he or Eileen would recount Father's homily. We'd all join in sharing what the readings meant to us; what was God trying to tell me, us, at this time in our lives, and share as well our thoughts on the homily—what it stirred in us. What a comfort to receive the Word and the Eucharist with such faithful friends! Along with this wonderful spiritual food, they brought us hot breakfast sandwiches and delicious coffee cakes and stayed and ate with us, sitting around our coffee table in the living room. More times than I remember, those Sunday mornings were what got me through the next few days.

Every third or fourth week, St. Peter's Folk Group (which, in better days, I was a part of) would join Tom and Eileen. A couple of times they even had to shovel their way in and out, but the weather never stopped them. Bernadette would bring her guitar, and we'd sing all the songs that they had sung at Mass that morning. Again, we shared on the day's readings and the homily as well as on all the breakfast foods, fruits and juices they brought with them—a real agape (love feast). Joanne and I never felt alone or separated from the community or God—these great people taking time out of their busy lives, made sure of that. It meant more than I can adequately express to be so connected and loved by my community. Like the words of that old song, Sundays will never be the same.

8

"You O Lord, are always my shield from danger; you give me victory and restore my courage. I call to the Lord for help and from his sacred hill he answers me."

—Psalm 3:3-4

8th email

Subject: God is our refuge & strength, a very present help in trouble. Psalm 46:2
Date: Thursday, August 21, 2003   11:17 a.m.

Dear Angels,

It's hard to keep believing, to keep reaching with your heart for the hem of his garment—to "speak life" on faith alone. The hot, humid weather was robbing my sweetheart of his strength and the little breath he had. And as it did, it crushed our spirits and we began to fall into fear and unbelief. We didn't stop praying or believing that God was with us; we just prayed less often and with less enthusiasm. We attended Mass less frequently; it was subtle, and we didn't even realize what was happening. ("Be on guard against the wiles and the snares of the devil".)

God in His everlasting love did not abandon us. He sent His angels to triumph over the spirit of despair and unbelief that was moving in on us—to "lift us up…and protect us in all of our ways…".

While we didn't recognize them at first, we see now that they were working powerfully right before and through the [NY area] Blackout in the unbelievable concern that our beautiful community of friends, family, neighbors expressed—in too many ways to note. There were the so very many calls from near and far, even from vacations; the uplifting news of our friend Tom's improvement and transfer to Helen Hayes Rehab Hospital; the love and generosity of dear, old friends who came and stayed a couple of days and ministered to us in ordinary and fun ways—they filled more than our stomachs. And it had to be the angels who pushed us and got us to the City to see The Man of LaMancha (the tickets were a gift from our son and we didn't want to disappoint him). The show was fantastic! It reminded us (planted the words in our hearts) "...to dream the impossible dream...to go where the brave dare not go, to reach with our last ounce of courage, to reach the unreachable star..." And for the first time, we'll be following our star through unchartered skies. We'll be relying heavily on your prayers.

Sometime soon, Bob will begin an experimental drug therapy, Actimmune, and we need you to stand strong with us in believing it will be the instrument God uses to perform the miracle we've all been praying for—restored lungs and long life.

Once again we feel anointed by the Precious Blood of Jesus (by His blood we have been saved). We're surrounded now with the spirit of truth. We know and believe our God speaks life into brokeness, that our Father is willing and able, that HIS WILL IS LIFE! And so thanks be to God and all of you, we're able to pick up our belief and believe again—onward and upward we go!!!

We love you with a renewed heart of thanksgiving,
    Joanne and Bobby

◆   ◆   ◆

People were wonderful to us—people we knew would be there for us and people we barely knew: men delivering oxygen to our home, hospital parking attendants, staff technicians and nurses. It seemed everyone treated us with care and kindness and confirmed for us that we were covered by prayer, held up on it's powerful wings by God's good people.

◆   ◆   ◆

People like Rick who during his busiest season and the hottest days of summer, dropped everything to respond to my cry for help; the heat and humidity was causing even more stress on Bobby's lungs. Rick had a team of men come right over and installed central air conditioning in our home in 5 hours, all the while smiling and saying, "Anything for the Wetzels".

Then there were two guys who made my life easier just by being the good men they are, Rich and George who live nearby. They made themselves available to us at a moment's notice and were always willing and happy to help in any way they could. This time they pulled our old, big inefficient wall A/C out of the Living Room wall and patched the gap it left. Our own sons don't live nearby, Rich and George were great substitutes.

And Joe S. an old "gold" friend who good naturedly drove us to out-of-the-way labs and offices in Manhattan where parking and managing a wheelchair would have been impossible without him. One would think we were doing him a favor instead of the other way around.

When simple, daily chores were getting too difficult to keep up with, our good neighbor, Jerry, was there to lighten the load. For instance, he moved the garbage pails out to the curb and brought them back empty. And when winter came, it was Jerry who kept our steps and walkway snow free most of the time.

And there was Eddie who, as an on-going prayer, had committed to give up smoking when Bobby was first diagnosed with IPF. The bright morning of the first heavy snowfall, we looked out the window to capture the beauty of it and beheld another vision of beauty. Eddie, Nancy (who was pregnant) and their two-year old son Jake, were shoveling our driveway, waving and smiling up at us.

My hairstylist, Jeanette, hearing that Bobby couldn't get out to the barber anymore and knowing I was no longer able to leave him, came by regularly and kept us both looking and feeling a whole lot better by her skill and generosity.

People thought of everything and anything to help us through our crisis. Friends and relatives came frequently and regularly with food and good cheer. And a few very thoughtful women, Barbara C., BettyLou and Michelle, took turns calling everyday to see if we needed something from the market or if there was anything else they could do to meet our needs and/or keep our spirits up.

Several times a week those many months, we received beautiful, inspirational cards and letters from either Barbara or Carole, encouraging us to stand strong in faith and on the promises of God. I looked forward to the mail and read and re-read their uplifting faith-building words. They weren't new to me, but I needed to be reminded of them now, as I watched my sweetheart's life slipping away.

The Lord graced us with so many caring, giving, beautiful people—always more than enough, who reflected God's faithfulness and everlasting love. Bobby so often marvelled at how blessed we were and how loved he felt. God was holding us close to His heart and even in the pain, we knew it and felt His protection.

9

"Trust in the Lord with all your heart and lean not on your own understanding, in all your ways acknowledge him, and he will direct you and crown your efforts with success."

—*Proverbs 3:5-6*

9th email

Subject: "…in all your ways acknowledge Him…"
Date: 9/18/2003 9:50 p.m.

To each and all of you who share our journey,

It's been a mostly good month—we've been believing and God's still willing and able. Let me tell you a little of how willing and able…

We met with Dr. Simonelli today (Columbia Presbyterian) and expressed our slowly growing concern that we hadn't received word from the drug company (Actimmune) and that precious time was being lost. From the doctor's careful response we hear his concern as well: not only that Bobby's condition may worsen but also that the delayed response could mean that Actimmune was not going to approve him for treatment.

At that low point (and out of the blue) I asked the doctor to please be open to God's promptings [on Bobby's behalf] because we were sure that God led us to him and will perform a miracle through him, and a whole lot of prayers were backing him up. He smiled softly, reached for my hand and said, "Sounds good to me." The routine exam continued with us going to the X-ray Department and returning later to drop off the x-ray.

We joined the doctor and his wife (receptionist) as they ate lunch. While reading the x-ray and saying there seemed to be no change since the March one (good news), the phone rang. "He's having lunch—no, no this is a priority", she mentioned a name and handed the phone to the doctor. He says, "Yes—yes—well you can talk to him, he's standing right here beside me" and hands Bobby the phone. "Yes—yes—that's wonderful, wonderful…(tears welling up in his eyes, so naturally in mine as well). It was the Drug Company Rep who proceeded to tell Bobby he was not only approved to take the drug (which will arrive at our home tomorrow, Friday), but also that they had contacted our insurance company to see if they could persuade them to pick up part of the $4000 monthly cost of the drug, with good results. (As a rule, Insurance Companies do not cover experimental drugs.) Now, hold onto your hats—this is gonna blow you away—our cost for the drugs will be a $10.00 copay a month!!!

We immediately and with certainty knew God was with us, that He was honoring our trust and acknowledgment, and further assuring us that yes, this drug is the way to go. We're filled anew with wonder and awe by our mighty God, our loving Father. To Him be all honor, glory and praise forever and ever!!!

Continue with us in praying and believing…

We love you,
Joanne and Bobby

◆   ◆   ◆

When I was on Actimmune about a month without any positive results, doubts of its effectiveness would occasionally arise in me. I was getting weaker, losing my appetite and struggling more for breath. Joanne was concerned that I might be getting discouraged and since she considered discouragement to be one of the devil's greatest tools, she prayed against the devil: "get thee behind me satan", and called on the Lord—"He who is in me is greater than that which is in the world."

Well the Lord came quickly to restore my spirit with what I call "Cornerstone Saturday". Cornerstone is a retreat that's been in our parish eight years. The retreat team shares and witnesses on their journey towards God and basically work for a year building community, developing a closer relationship with the Lord and preparing talks. I was involved in the process, helping the witnesses develop and share their story.

When the retreat went on, I was too ill to be there. It was the first one I missed, and though Joanne said, "You'll be there next year", and I said things like" I'll be with you in spirit" and "I'll be praying for you guys", inside myself I felt a blow—another reminder that I really couldn't be one of the guys anymore. The fact was, I was going from bad to worse and while I was grateful for the eight retreats I had been a part of, I thought my Cornerstone days were over.

Well much to my joy and their good character, these guys proved me wrong. When the parish retreat was over, Richie (a strength to us throughout), says: "the guys want to come over some Saturday". They'd put together a condensed version of the retreat and wanted to share their finished stories with me. What a much needed shot in the arm that experience was, a great day. We laughed, cried and prayed, and as always, ended with food and fun and the comforting feeling of God's embrace.

◆   ◆   ◆

10th email

Subject: Pray, Speak, Choose—LIFE…
Date: 11/10/2003   8:21 p.m.

Here's the update. Bobby's been on the experimental drug, Actimmune, about six weeks. We haven't seen any improvement, if anything, he appears to be losing ground. Seeing him slow down, laboring more for breath, and needing more oxygen, causes us to lose heart and oftentimes to grow fearful that God's plan may not be what we are praying for—restored lungs and long life.
However, we are reminded time and again, that GOD'S WILL IS FOR LIFE—that HE IS WILLING AND ABLE to crush any disease. So today we step out in faith and decide again to choose life. We rebuke this deadly disease in the name of Jesus, to say to it, in the light of the tremendous POWER OF GOD, the power of Jesus Christ who triumphed over death, and the Power of the Holy Spirit poured out on us: Pulmonary Fibrosis, you are powerless here—God has already won the victory—He will have the final word, and to the glory of God, we will have a miracle!

So we ask you tonight to pray positively daily—to stay focused on how pow-erful our God is, how nothing is impossible with Him, how He is working to healing and life—performing a miracle here and now in our midst. We praise you and thank you Lord for the powerful way you are working in our lives—for ever-renewed faith and increased intimacy—for "wonderful comrades"—for the strength in believing together. Amen.

10

"I am still confident of this: I will see the goodness of the Lord in the land of the living. Wait for the Lord; be strong and take heart and wait for the Lord."

—*Psalm 27:13-14*

I marvel when I recognize a way God reaches us that doesn't appear to be a direct path. Certainly it's not because he doesn't know an easier way; it's likely because we often "don't see the forest for the trees". Several times during our faith journey, he reached us through a chance encounter, not necessarily our own.

This time it was through Barbara S., a good friend and kindred spirit who called me from California extremely excited about what had just transpired on the plane ride there. She was seated across from a man reading a bible, who turned out to be a pastor returning from a speaking engagement in Detroit. Being Barbara, she asked what he had spoken about and he was happy to tell her at length.

His topic was faith and prayer. He spoke about praying, expecting to receive what you pray for, and went on to quote passages in scripture that instructed us to do so. Before long, Barbara knew without a doubt the message was for Bobby who years before, told anyone who'd listen to pray with expectant faith, thanking God in advance for answering the request. He had been successful and confident in praying that way then, and she knew that's how we were praying now for his miracle. She also knew that some of our relatives and friends questioned whether we were in denial, not facing the reality of Bob's condition and God's ways. I wondered too at times, but kept choosing to believe in spite of the circumstances.

Barbara hearing the pastor's name was Branch, was reassured that her meeting him was God's plan. She was traveling with her daughter, also a Branch. Her enthusiasm was contagious and I hung on every word and scribbled notes as she continued. The pastor's message, in a nutshell, was: have faith and confidence in God's Word; Do not be afraid; believe and persevere in prayer.

The scripture passages he quoted were Mark 4:35-41 where Jesus speaks to the storm and says to his Apostles, "Why are you so afraid? How is it that you have no faith?" Hebrews 3:1-6 about the faithfulness of Moses and Jesus in their Father's house—"And we are in His house, as long as we cling to our hope with confidence that we glory in."

He told her we have to speak to the storms in our lives, the storms being the troubles or pain we have. We have to speak to them while we are in the midst of them, with confidence and faith in God's word until the storm ends.

Barbara listened eagerly to his every word (as I was to hers) and continued with Matthew 11:23 "Have faith in God. I tell you solemnly if anyone says to this mountain 'get up and throw yourself into the sea,' with no hesitation in his heart but believing that what he says will happen, it will be done for him". The mountain being whatever we're battling now. Mark 11:24 "I tell you therefore: everything you ask and pray for, believe that you have it already, and it will be yours".

As Christians we have to walk and act in confidence. Confidence is trusting, relying and assuring in your mind that what you are about is based on God's will and not on Satan. Acting confidently means no doubts, and firm trust that what you ask for you will receive. Further he cautioned that we should also speak that way—words projecting faith and trust. Jeremiah 32:26-27 "The word of Yahweh was addressed to me as follows, 'See I am Yahweh, the God of all mankind: is anything impossible to me?' Again talking about unwavering faith being able to move mountains.

Then Deuteronomy 31:6-8 where Moses is speaking: "Be strong, stand firm; you are going with this people into the land Yahweh swore to their fathers he would give them; you are to give it into their possession. Yahweh himself will lead you; he will be with you; he will not fail you or desert you. Have no fear, do not be disheartened by anything."

She relayed all this over the phone as soon and as completely as she could in order to build us up. We were both flying on God's love when we hung up. I knew coincidence didn't bring Barbara and Pastor Branch together, rather it was God's plan to strengthen us and keep us strong in faith. My hope was at a high and my faith affirmed—I couldn't wait to share this powerful sign and message with Bobby.

But wait, there's more. As the pastor prepared to leave the plane, he handed Barbara a book, How Faith Works by Frederick K.C. Price, Ph.D., which she gave to Bobby. It affirms his message and instructs the readers to build up their faith in community with others who believe, and to avoid naysayers. Oh how true we knew that to be. From the very beginning of this ordeal, we needed and relied on the strength and affirmation of strong believers, and praise God, we were surrounded by them. When the few well-meaning people who seemed to only see the facts talked with me, I either changed the subject or dismissed in my mind what they implied. They saw facts, not truth. The facts said: Bobby's dying. The truth was: God's word is telling us His will for him is life.

11

"May the Lord bless you from Zion all the days of your life; may you see the prosperity of Jerusalem, and may you live to see your children's children."

—Psalm 128:5-6

What is it about grandchildren that they can evoke joy and melancholy at the same time? Being with them during my illness was like that—bittersweet. I don't know why, but somehow the depth of my feelings for them often took me by surprise. They lived on Long Island and could only visit with their parents on weekends.

Matthew the oldest, 13, saw things weren't going well. Always quiet, he seemed cautious and concerned now as well. Zachary, 11, was hesitant when approaching me and seemed uneasy too; he was handling it by trying to act like nothing had changed. Rachel, 12 (going on 30), always very affectionate and verbal, would ask how I felt and tell me how good I looked. She'd hug and kiss me and several times each visit, she'd tell me she loved me. Her brother, Michael, 10, would follow Rachel's lead asking how I felt and saying he loved me. He'd follow that up with some antics to make me laugh, which wasn't unlike his usual behavior.

And then there was Julia, she was 5, our baby, but smart and sensitive. She'd walk in slowly, hesitantly and wait for me to put my arms out, then she'd run over, smiling and give me a big hug and kiss. She knew Poppy wasn't the same, and didn't like it. Sometimes she'd say, "you can do it Poppy, you can play with me" or "come inside and color, come on."

I always wanted to see them and liked knowing they were around, but it was hard on me emotionally, and as the disease progressed, it got harder on them too. They'd come in and over to the couch, "Hi Poppy", "Hello Poppy", a hug, a kiss and off they'd go to play video or computer games, go outside to play ball or catch frogs or lightening bugs or later, play in the snow. They all knew to keep their distance if they had even a hint of a cold; they'd wear surgical masks in the living room, wash their hands vigorously with Purell and save the hugs and kisses for the next time.

During many of those visits I'd suddenly find my eyes misting over and all the things I might miss in their growing up would flood my mind. There was a good possibility I wouldn't be around as they went through the milestones that most families celebrate and mark as part of their family history, and knowing that wrung my heart.

At times, their education would come to mind, missing high school and college years. Other times, their spiritual development and receiving their sacraments; Eucharist, Confirmation and Marriage. They were great kids and I knew they'd mature into wonderful young men and women, and I wanted to see it—to be there when they went on to take life partners and have children of their own and continue the Wetzel circle of life.

It wasn't something I dwelled on or was morbid about, in fact, I'm not sure anyone except Joanne, noticed. The thoughts were fleeting but the feelings were always just under the surface, kept in check. And during most embraces, more times than not, I'd have to blink back the tears.

As the disease continued to progress, breathing became more and more difficult even with oxygen. It got to a point where I was conscious of almost every breath I took. Nothing else mattered except that next breath.

The only thing that seemed to help was reading. When I read, I could get into a rhythm and get to what I called an "at rest" condition where I was less aware of breathing. I had enjoyed reading all my life and was thankful that even now, it provided me some relief.

By winter, breathing took up all my energy and I was living what I had learned at Rehab, that unlike a normal person who uses 100 calories a day to breath, someone with lung disease uses up to 1000 calories a day just to breath. No wonder I was losing so much weight (62 lbs. by Feb.). This is not a diet, however, that I'd recommend to anyone.

I moved from the bedroom to the living room to the den and back to the bedroom at night. I held back on going to the bathroom because it just took too much effort. Joanne bathed and shaved me either in bed or beside it and I used a urinal and commode whenever I could. When I did try to get to the bathroom, I'd have to crank up the oxygen to 15 liters and allow myself lots of time to get there.

I stopped coming to the table to eat because it required too much energy to move from one room to another. Our meals were now eaten in the living room or the den. Breathing was much more important than eating. I couldn't even eat a small piece of candy, the size given out at Halloween, because chewing it would take my breath away.

I tried to keep the little energy I had to continue going to Rehab three times a week. Drs. Simonelli and Bartel continually stressed the importance of walking and exercise and I was determined to do as much or as little as I could. I knew I couldn't do it on my own. I needed the professional expertise and dedicated support I received at Helen Hayes Hospital. Another blessing—it was only five minutes away, practically in our backyard. God had seen to everything.

As my health continued to deteriorate and it was obvious that I was getting worse, I mentioned to Joanne that it didn't look like the experimental drug was having any effect—she was having the same disheartening thoughts but seemed more confident that God would intervene. I told her, "If you believe, I'll believe".

12

"May the God of Hope fill you with all joy and peace as you trust in Him, so that you may overflow with hope by the power of the Holy Spirit."

—Romans 15:13

11ᵗʰ email

Subject: AWESOME GOD
Date: 12/8/2003   12:42 p.m.

Hope you had a wonderful Thanksgiving and are enjoying your Christmas preparations. Our Thanksgiving was wonderful. We went to Mark & Kathy's on Wednesday and spent the holiday with all our children and our Wetzel family (brothers, sisters, nieces, nephews, etc.). However, by night-time and the trip home my sweetheart was having a rough time breathing even with the oxygen. Friday we called the doctor and Wednesday, December 3ʳᵈ he was hospitalized for testing. Just maybe it was something other than the pulmonary fibrosis that was setting him back. Thursday night Dr. Simonelli gave us the test results. They weren't good; there was nothing else—it's the disease progressing. The experimental drug he's taking doesn't appear to be stopping the progression as we had hoped it would. Our hearts were sinking fast—and then came Jesus "…walking on the water…".

The doctor followed up the bad news with—IF Bobby was willing, and IF he did well on some further tests, they'll "make an exception" for him and put him into Columbia's lung transplant program. We had been told from the very beginning that he wasn't eligible, he was well beyond the cut-off age. But God made a path where there was none…He lifts us up…He renews our hope…My spirit immediately began to soar and praise God; easy for me in good health, not for Bobby. He said we needed to pray about it.

The first reading I randomly opened to was Jeremiah 32:26 "Then the word of God came…I am the Lord, the God of all mankind. Is anything too hard for me?" Later, Deuteronomy 30:19 "This day I call heaven and earth as witnesses against you that I have set before you life and death, blessings and curses. Now choose life…"

And so we are going forward, realizing it can be a long, arduous road, but believing that wherever it leads, whatever tomorrow brings, God is already there. We're home now, waiting for the next tests to be scheduled and working at trusting Him completely—He has a plan for our lives, and right now, that's all we need to know. Deuteronomy 31:6 "Be strong and courageous. Do not be afraid or terrified…for the Lord your God goes before you; he will never leave you nor forsake you." Praise God—stand strong on His Word with us. He is mighty, merciful and faithful—beyond all our expectations and understanding!

Now if we sound like God is doing a great job carrying us, it's because He is, but please know that it's YOUR ARMS He's using. We need you and are eternally grateful for all the ways you love us.

We love you too,
Joanne & Bobby

P.S. Just got a call, Bobby is scheduled for a Heart Catheterization this Friday, December 12ᵗʰ at 1 p.m. Laurie & Anthony will be getting our new grandson then—got to be a day the Lord has made! Please keep us in prayer.

◆   ◆   ◆

When Dr. Simonelli told us—me, Joanne and our son, Scott, that there was a possibility of a lung transplant if I could pass some tests, Joanne and Scott were thrilled. Me, I withdrew. I remember Joanne saying "it's your decision" and I replied, "we'll have to pray about it".

The idea of a lung transplant came almost as a shock to me. It never entered my mind—I didn't think it was an option. At one of my early visits with Doctor Simonelli, he told us I was too old to be considered for a transplant. At the time, it was the furthest thing from my mind and if given the choice then, I believe I would have said no. Of course, the disease hadn't progressed very far. I was without oxygen, functioning pretty normally and believing I was gonna beat this disease. Things were a lot different now.

When I was alone that night, I asked myself why I didn't say yes immediately and realized I was afraid. I had visions of myself on a hospital table with my chest cut open and all kinds of blood and guts coming out. I wasn't afraid of dying, I was afraid of being operated on which seemed kind of strange to me because I'd had major lung surgery before and it hadn't worried me at all.

I said a few prayers, didn't receive any deep revelations or inspirations, but decided to go for it. I knew I really didn't have any other choice.

Joanne was already in my hospital room when I awoke the next morning. She was relaxed and confident that the outcome of my prayers were the same as hers and that I'd choose a chance at life.

Dr. Simonelli didn't appear surprised when we advised him that we'd like to go for it. I think he may have already put the testing process in motion, and advised the first test would be a heart catheterization the following week. Apparently to be considered at all for a lung transplant, I'd have to be heart healthy.

He wanted to know more about my past history and why I was taking several heart medications when he didn't see any heart problems. The catheterization results would determine if we could proceed.

◆   ◆   ◆

While Dr. Simonelli had already signed Bobby's discharge papers, he asked us not to leave the hospital; he was hoping we'd get a visit from Dr. Joshua Sonett, Director of the Lung Transplant Program. He'd been paging him all morning and thought if he was in the hospital, he'd stop by to meet us. He wanted him to see Bobby, the person, not just paperwork: numbers and medical reports.

Shortly after, we met Dr. Sonett for the first time. Finally a face to go with the voice that answered my prayer and gave me hope seven months before when I was looking for an appointment with "the best" doctor in the pulmonary field. He looked like a kid to us, exuding energy and confidence. He sat on the bed next to Bobby, pulled no punches, was direct and to the point. Even if Bobby passed all the initial tests, and got on the Transplant list, he'd have to remain strong in order to stay on it. The normal average waiting time once on the list was 12—18 months and, as time passed, he'd have to retest. Being older, he'd be at a disadvantage in fighting off any infections, viruses, the flu, etc. and less resilient as well. He wanted us to go into this knowing what we were agreeing to. It would be a long, tough road with no guarantees. While this was the message he wanted to get across and did, I knew in my heart that he was considering him despite his age, and that Dr. Sonett once again, was an answer to our prayers.

◆   ◆   ◆

We are so grateful for Dr. Simonelli, his wonderful care and dedication, who despite my poor heart history and my age, went out of his way to push my case with Dr. Sonett; and for Dr. Sonett's "yes" and brilliant surgical skills. We thank God from the bottom of our hearts for both of these good men and their cooperation, knowingly or not, with God's plan to perform a miracle for us!

13

"Let us hold unswervingly to the hope we profess for he who promised is faithful."

—Hebrews 10:23

An unforseen side benefit of keeping everyone aware of what was going on with me and asking to be remembered in their prayers, was a strong, unified, prayer community. Paul and Bernadette held a prayer service for us in their home and others requested special prayers amongst themselves, even sending out emails.

◆   ◆   ◆

Subject: Bob's Breath Prayer
Thurs., Dec.11, 2003

"More things are wrought by prayer than this world dreams of."—Alfred Lord Tennyson

As many of you may know from Richie's email earlier this week, Bob will be undergoing a procedure (heart catheterization) tomorrow (Friday) at 1:00 p.m. Joanne's daughter-in-law Kathy will be with her at Columbia tomorrow while the procedure is being performed. It's an outpatient procedure so Bob and Joanne will be home tomorrow night.

In speaking with Barbara C. on Tuesday, she mentioned something called a "Breath Prayer." Very briefly, a breath prayer can be a word, phrase or short sentence. The name Breath Prayer comes from the Hebrew word "ruach' which can be translated as "wind", "breath," or "spirit." Praying the breath prayer reminds us that we share God's breath.

We would like to join Bob and Joanne and, of course, their whole family in praying Bob's breath prayer at 1:00 p.m. tomorrow.

Bob's breath prayer is: HOLY SPIRIT, BATHE HIS LUNGS IN YOUR HEALING LIGHT.

It takes less than a minute to repeat this prayer five—ten times. We all know the power of prayer and in this way we can ALL be there tomorrow at 1:00 p.m. with Bob and Joanne.

If I have missed anyone that would like to receive this message (and I'm sure I have), please let them know about Bob's breath prayer.

Love,   AnneMarie

◆   ◆   ◆

I had been under my local cardiologist's care for several years and was being medicated and monitored for Angina and the ill effects of a silent heart attack. We were also going into this test aware that I hadn't done too well on my latest nuclear stress test (October 2002), but the community's attempt to storm the gates of heaven at the scheduled procedure time touched our hearts and strengthened our resolve to trust the Lord for good test results.

Knowing all our communities, people everywhere, were lifting us up in prayer, was a tremendous comfort and encouragement.

The breath prayer was used many times over, with slight variations, depending on what test or procedure I was having at the time, and always I felt safer and more hopeful because of it.

Once again God showed Himself strong with the favorable results of the heart catheterization which indicated I was heart healthy. Blockage was normal and minimal for my age and my pressure was very good. As far as the team cardiologist was concerned, I was a good candidate for a lung transplant.

Having passed that big hurdle, we approached the next tests with a positive attitude thinking there would be only a few more less significant tests and a short time before I would get on the List.

That good news was immediately followed by receiving news right there in the hospital (via cell phone), that Laurie and Anthony had been given custody of Baby Daniel and he was home in Tennessee with them. There was a lot of rejoicing in our hearts—surely this was a day the Lord had made. Here He was again, blessing us abundantly. How could we lose heart with a Father who continually gives good gifts like this!

14

"You have changed my sadness into a joyful dance; and surrounded me with joy."

—*Psalm 30:11*

Christmas was always my favorite holiday. Like a kid, I couldn't wait
for it to come. As soon as Thanksgiving was over, I'd start on Christmas
preparations. The tree would go up, lights would be put on the house
(and Joanne would say I was turning them on too early). I'd have illu-
minated deer prancing on the lawn and fabric-mache santas all over the
house, and of course, a large flag that proclaimed "Jesus is the Heart of
the Season".

But this year wasn't like any other year. I didn't have the breath or the
strength to decorate anything. Any sort of movement on my part was
exhausting. I couldn't get to the shed to get the tree and wouldn't have
been able to carry it in if I could. My son, Scott, brought the tree in,
and with his children Rachel and Michael, got it up and in good shape.
Later my son-in-law, Anthony, re-strung the strands of lights that were
out. I have close to three thousand lights on my tree and the ornaments
have been picked with great interest and care, as well as the ones we've
received over the years. Usually I'd decorate the tree and Joanne finished it off placing the tree-top Angel and gold bows and streamers on
it, and I loved it all.

So now the tree was up and the lights were on, but it still had to be decorated and there was no way I could do that either. Old friends, Catherine and Joey, and cousins, Johnny and Dolores, called and offered to decorate for us on one of their many visits. They came up December 16th and even with the old familiar Christmas Carols playing softly in the background, it was like a strange scene out of a comedy show, only I wasn't laughing.

Joey and Johnny were up and down retrieving boxes of ornaments and decorations from the attic. Catherine and Dolores were opening the boxes and placing tree decorations here and other decorations there, admiring everything and, not knowing where things went, as well as in the hopes of keeping me a vital part of it, asking, "Where did I want this" and "Where did that go?"

Joey and Johnny then decorated the tree, and Joanne unwrapped and put my Santa collection in it's customary place. Everyone was trying hard to be cheerful and make it a joyful experience when, in reality, it was very painful for me. As I watched from the couch, I was reminded that my role was reduced to that of an observer, not a participant—I saw life slipping through my fingers and it took all my energy to keep a stiff upper lip. At the end of the day, the tree and the house looked great, like Christmases past. But for me, the most important element was missing—an energizing, joyful spirit.

Joanne continued holiday preparations and couldn't wait until Laurie got home from Tennessee with her special gift this year. While I was looking hopefully forward to that visit too, Christmas menus and gifts didn't hold my interest, all I seemed to care about these days was breathing and being able to put one foot in front of the other.

Laurie and Anthony arrived home the night of December 19th with their adopted baby, Daniel, who was four months old. It was the first time the family was getting to see him and we were all gathered together excitedly awaiting their arrival. I had previously, very sadly thought there was a good chance that Laurie might never become a mother. And more recently, that I probably wouldn't be here to see it, if or when she did. She and Anthony had been trying for so long to conceive and although they were told nothing was wrong with either of them, it just didn't happen.

Well God had different plans. They were in the process of adopting a baby girl from China when Laurie received a Word at a prayer gathering in December 2002 that she'd have a baby before the following Christmas [2003]. She and Anthony were thrilled and thought their paperwork was going to miraculously speed through and they wouldn't have to wait the customary 18-24 months for their baby.

That "following" Christmas was getting very close and while all their paperwork had made it to China, it still wasn't approved. It didn't seem possible that they'd get their baby anytime soon. Still they believed that the Word they received was from God and He would work it out. And He did.

One day, seemingly out of nowhere, a friend of Anthony's called and asked if they would be interested in adopting a baby boy. They received Daniel the same day I received the news that my heart was fine, December 12th—it was a great day for the family. They finally had their baby. Even if I might not be here to see him or share any of her milestones with him or the little girl they were still waiting for, she had her baby, and I thanked God for that.

The reality of it however didn't hit me then. It wasn't until she came into the living room with Daniel in her arms that it hit me. I took one look at them, kissed Daniel and held Laurie tightly in my arms for about five minutes. I couldn't let her go. I heard moaning and sobbing and realized it was me. I was crying my eyes out. All the fear and sadness I'd experienced thinking I'd never live to see this moment washed away. And while everyone in the room was crying, the tears brought healing and became rivers of joy. It didn't seem to matter anymore if I never experienced more of her motherhood than this—right now this was enough. Daniel with his dimpled, smiling face brought what we had been lacking—the joyful spirit of Christmas. What a truly awesome God we have who gives us more than we even hope for.

And then it was Christmas Eve. Our plans for a family dinner were thwarted because of family colds and flu. With my diseased lungs and compromised immune system, I couldn't take any chances. We were sitting alone in the den when we heard Christmas carols coming from outside. Joanne looked out the window and told me the Folk Group was out there singing. She ran to open wide the front door as I slowly made my way to the inside front steps and sat there looking out at the whole group with their children standing in the rain, singing their hearts out. It was overwhelming. I could barely speak, all I could do was cry as I felt wrapped in a blanket of God's love. See I will not forget you, I've sent an early gift, a treasure, from the Magi.

◆   ◆   ◆

While Christmas day itself was quiet, the spirit of it was alive in our hearts and carried over to the following Saturday when we were able to have our traditional Christmas celebration with the whole family. There was the usual Prime Rib dinner with all the trimmings and Poppy, having a pretty good day, was miraculously able to carry out our family tradition of reading the story of the Baby Jesus' birth to the family before gift opening. Yes, the Lord had come, God was with us and brought us above our everyday struggles to a place of cheer and peace.

15

"Do not fear, for I am with you; do not be dismayed for I am your God. I will strengthen you and help you; I will uphold you with my righteous right hand."

—Isaiah 41:10

Early in the New Year, during Laurie's holiday visit with us, she received a prophetic word via email from a friend praying for us in Tennessee.

Dear Laurie,
I think I might have heard something from the Lord on your dad's behalf…The Lord reminded me about the story of Moses defeating the Amalekites (Exodus 17:8). I felt the Lord was saying that Moses is symbolic of your father, Aaron and Hur are symbolic of those standing with him in prayer, and the Amalekites are symbolic of the "world" and the demonic forces coming against your family…I believe God has an encouraging word for him: STAND STRONG, the battle isn't over yet, but it will be soon, and it will be a victorious one!
Love,
Tina

Encouraging indeed!

◆   ◆   ◆

A "short time" to get on the list dragged on from December through the whole month of January, and the "few tests" turned into many. The initial Evaluation and Interviews didn't happen until January 12th but had a positive outcome—it was determined that I was a lot stronger than my age. So let the tests begin—there was a Chemical Stress Test, Urine Creatinine Clearance, a Colonoscopy, Bone Density Test and Upper GI Series as well as a Lung Perfusion Scan, an Ultrasound of the Carotid and of course, the dreaded Six Minute Walk. All these tests/procedures at different times and different locations. All at a time when I needed a wheel chair for any mobility, and getting out of the house into the car took about 45 minutes and every bit of strength and breath I had. How could I do it?

It seemed that every time we thought the transplant team had all they needed to put me on the Transplant List, the doctors wanted one more test. A lot of time was passing, and I was getting anxious. Remembering that Dr. Sonett had expressed the importance of getting me on the list ASAP—"in two weeks" and seven weeks had already passed, was discouraging, but didn't outweigh our thankfulness over being considered at all.

My condition was deteriorating rapidly, I had large oxygen reservoirs in 3 rooms of my house, a concentrator in another and portable tanks and masks all over, even in the car. After examining me during one of our visits, Dr. Sonett said I needed a transplant in 3—9 months. That was already a whole lot less than the average waiting time of a year to eighteen months. I thought: "I have to get on that list fast, and it better be less than three because I'm not making nine."

◆   ◆   ◆

12th email

Subject: "Nothings impossible [too hard] with God."
Date: 1/11/2004   2:53p.m.

Hi,

Appreciate your prayers and try to let you know outcomes as quickly as we do, so we can experience together the joy of answered prayer.

The conclusion reached Friday by Columbia P.H.'s Lung Transplant Team is that Bobby's stronger and healthier than his age—the evaluation went very well. How could it not: we were covered with a blanket of prayers and protected by the Precious Blood of Jesus.

A few tests (seemingly insignificant) remain and are planned for some-time within the next 7—12 days. They expect Bobby will officially be on the Transplant List in two weeks. We're not surprised, but we are full of praise and thanksgiving. Our God made a path where there was none and has now placed us firmly on it.

We were interviewed by the Transplant Team Friday, the 9th, from 9 to 2:30, one doctor at a time. They were wonderful, young, caring peo-ple—committed to the Transplant Program and to reaching the best deci-sion for my sweetheart. The toughest part of the evaluation was the Six-Minute Walk. Fortunately they kind of sprang it on us. Before we had time for concern, Bobby was up and walking. They expressed an understanding of how difficult it would be for him, as well as the importance of pushing himself and completing it. Afterwards they said he needed to finish 600 steps. With the help of God who he called on the whole time, he completed 1012! While he was physically exhausted from the ordeal, our spirits were peaceful and carefree through the day-long process. (The fruit of many prayers.)

We felt surrounded by love and had gotten several calls from our "kids" before and even during our time there—sharing love, words and signs from the Lord for us: "Jesus stretched out his hand, touched him, and said, I DO WILL IT. Be made clean." And, "The angels of the Lord are encamped around those who fear the Lord, and they will deliver them." The Blessed Mother and Angels were sent to take our troubles away, and words from contemporary Christian music encouraged us: "You raise me up so I can stand on mountains....I am strong when I am on your shoulders, you raise me up to more than I can be." [and do]

Throughout many of the interviews, the importance of a strong support system was stressed. We were warned not to try to do this alone—it's not an easy road to travel and offers no guarantees. They wanted us to name people who we could count on to be with us through the long process. In responding we showed them 2 group pictures, one of us with our kids and grandkids, and one of us with our church family. They were deeply impressed, and we were aware again how blessed we are by all of you—your love and presence in our lives, your commitment to continue sharing life—this journey with us. He gives wonderful family, friends, prayer "comrades" to us. He's absolutely amazing. He's thought of everything! "Do not fear, for I am with you; do not be dismayed, for I am your God. I will strengthen you and help you; I will uphold you with my righteous right hand." Isaiah 41:10

So at this point, it's Bobby's job to push himself to exercise and stay strong, ours to keep praying and believing, and God's to get the lungs. Our trust and confidence remains strong in the Lord to supply them at the perfect time.

Lots of love and prayers for a joyful, blessed year—
Joanne and Bobby

I want to share some of the community responses to hearing Bobby did so well on the Six-Minute walk:

"Oh my God!!!!!!!!!!!!!!!!!!! I am soooo relieved…I am soooo grateful…I knew it! All things are possible!!!!!!!!!!! I know that but sometimes you get so scared…Boy He/She surely loves his Boyo Son Bobby!!!!!!!!!!! He/She is giving us some lesson in Faith and the power of Prayer…god I wish it didn't have to be so intense or I wish he/she used someone else as a vehicle…for this extravaganza!!! Well Uncle Bobby always had our attention…so I guess it was a good choice…Thank you for keeping me in the loop…you have become so present in my life…I imagine you are so present in everyone's lives…So keep writing me…I love you both and feel like I am witnessing a miracle…not that lil every day sort but a BIG TIME MIRACLE…so keep it up…you may even get me back to church (oh God I never left) I love you!!! Kathleen" (Suffolk County, NY)

"Our hearts ache to be with you—but we are there in prayer and spirit—ALL DAY. Prayers are coming from far and wide. Friends and coworkers lift him up in prayer. All that Bobby has given to his Christian community is coming back to him ten-fold. Who is blessed more—Bobby or us? All of our Christian friends and the staff I work with are praying for him. Breathe on him breath of life.
Much love,
Mike & Dottie"   (North Carolina)

Your walk through this horribly difficult struggle has been inspirational to so many—including us. You are really being a testament to God's grace and power. We can't wait to dance a jig of rejoicing when the victory is complete!

All our love,

Laurie & Anthony

16

"Morning by morning, O Lord, you hear my voice; morning by morning, I lay my requests before you and wait in expectation."

—Psalm 5:3

Dear Sisters & Brothers in Christ,

Please see Joanne's note below and offer your prayers for these loyal and faithful servants of God who continue to guide and inspire us as they walk this journey in faith.
May God Bless & Keep You and those You Love,
Richie

◆   ◆   ◆

13th email

Subject: STAND STRONG the battle isn't over yet…it will be victorious!
Date: January 28, 2004

Apparently we jumped the gun on getting on the Lung Transplant List "after a few tests". Seems that more and more tests were added to the list of "must haves". However, as of yesterday, Tuesday, January 27th, Bobby completed all of the required tests/procedures. The reports/results of all the tests, as well as notes from doctors who examined him and interviewed us at the

Evaluation, will be compiled and hopefully, presented to the Lung Trans-plant Team this Friday, January 30th. (Another good sign; our son Chris' Birthday.)

So here we are again, asking for your earnest, heartfelt prayers.
"I urge, then, first of all, that requests, prayers, intercession and thanksgiv-ing be made for everyone…"(Timothy 2:1)…and especially for Bobby this Friday morning.

We lift the Transplant Team up and pray the Holy Spirit will touch them with his love and release his power, softening their hearts and opening them to God's will on Bobby's behalf. "Let us approach the throne of grace with confidence, so that we may receive mercy and find grace to help us in our time of need." (Hebrews 4:16).

How blessed are we that we "approach the throne of grace with confidence" with so many! Surely He will pour out His mercy, as He has His love, on us. We feel ourselves more and more these days, held "in the palm of His hand"—through you.

All our love and gratitude,
Joanne and Bobby

Responses from the community:

"Hi Joanne & Bob,
The battle is about to be won! Don't know if Barbara told you about her being prayed over for Bob at the prayer meeting and her experience, but I wanted to let you know as I (Marie) had my hand on her as I closed my eyes the vision of what I didn't know what it was at first it came to me that

what seemed like a pure white tubular streak was a picture of Bob's new lung. To me it was a vision of what is to be and praise God it will come to pass. I just feel sure of this and I just needed to share that with you. You lovers are such a witness of saints that love the Lord beyond anyone I know and you call me forth to be more. When I hear your love of Him it calls me to pray more to love Him more and know Him more. And I just wanted to thank you for your faithfulness. You're children of God and my brother and sister in Christ who I admire abundantly and am sooooo grateful you are in our lives. You are so very precious to us and we just need to tell you that. We miss you terribly down here and it is like a part of our body is hurting so much. And until this battle is over we will never give up the pouring out of prayers. There have been mornings when it has been hard to get out of bed to go and be fed the body and blood of Jesus. But what gets me going is knowing the two of you would pay anything to be where you have the freedom and physical ability to have that privilege at this time. So know we are going for you and that is how we can show our love for you and support you at this time of crisis. We love you and embrace you.
Marie & Al" (Florida)

"Amen! Amen! That's wonderful and we receive it!! Get that tubular white streak a.k.a. lung, here now Lord!! Amen
Laurie" (Tennessee)

"You are in our prayers every day. Those who love you are storming the gates of heaven seeking and expecting that one of his "Kings Kids" will be healed. His miracles are limitless.
Our love is with you both. Praise God!
Joan and Jerry" (Queens, New York)

And then another prophetic word from Kelly in Tennessee:

"James W. Goll: 'There will be Open Doors in 2004'
This is a good website—about prophetic voices. National & International. Part of the messages for 2004, repeatedly occurring, is one of the tremendous healings that God is releasing in 2004. Here's part of one of them:

"I was taken in the Spirit recently into a room called "Heaven's Healing Rooms". As I entered past the doors into this room filled with the brilliant healing presence of God, I saw creative miracles. Body parts were in this room. I saw eyes, hearts, hands, legs, lungs—you name it—it was there. In 2004 "missing body parts" will be released—both for the spiritual body of Christ and for natural bodies needing creative miracles."

Amen! Amen! We say, Amen!"

◆   ◆   ◆

God seemed to be bombarding us with signs that He was working on it and was generous in letting us know He was.

17

"I wait for you O Lord; you will answer O Lord my God."

—*Psalm 38:15*

As Bobby's condition worsened, more and more of his care fell on me. It never was too much for me, I was happy to be able to relieve a little of his struggle in any way I could.

I saw that God had prepared me for these hardest days of my life in so many ways. Books I read, a heart for scripture, prayer and life experiences I'd had—all there to fall back on now. I remembered a phrase from our marriage vows about sacrificial love—"that true love could make it a joy". Now 46 years later, I was experiencing that truth.

The holy name of Jesus was almost always on my lips and I called on Mother Theresa and St. Theresa as I tried to follow their example and do everything with love, to have Bobby feel surrounded, engulfed in love. Each of the many times throughout the day and night I had to adjust his oxygen levels, I'd pray that portion of the Divine Chaplet: "for the sake of His sorrowful Passion, have mercy on my sweetheart [on us] and on the whole world."

Doing for him was easy, standing by helpless, seeing him lose so much ground, and energy was hard. Especially during his Rehab sessions at Helen

Hayes. I couldn't bear to see him drawing on every ounce of waning strength and breath to do less and less of the exercises and the walking that we knew was necessary to stay on the lung transplant list. It was beyond painful for me and I'd have to stop watching, leave the room on some pretense and pull myself together before returning.

Just getting to the hospital and back was an unbelievable ordeal—necessitating changing oxygen masks and tanks, and dealing with the effects the cold weather had on the oxygen hoses. And that was after managing the tedious struggle to get down (and then up) the stairs, and getting into a wheel chair and then into (and out of) the car. With the help of God, through the power of positive prayer, he was able to keep going. The only day he said, "I can't go today", and I knew he couldn't, was the day before our miracle.

He was always wonderful—never complaining, moody or unpleasant. As his health continued to fail, he became quieter and a little more withdrawn but he never fell into the "poor me's". The few times he cried then was not for himself, but for me. That he had become too heavy a burden for me to carry.

So how do you do all that has to be done when your heart is breaking and your sweetheart's life is slipping away day by day? You stay as close as you can to Jesus and to your beloved so that all the love that's spilling out falls on him and brings you both, the peace that surpasses all understanding. And you let the people the Lord sends into your life carry you.

Many times in those last 3 months, I felt like we were suspended in another dimension, somewhere between heaven and earth. I thought the angels must be holding us up on their wings. There was pain and suffering there, but predominantly, love and peace. I often remembered the words of an old poster Laurie brought home from college that said, "God has a plan for my [our] life. That's all I need to know". It was enough for me. The truth was crystal clear: no matter what the next moment or days brought, God was already there with our miracle and we were forever safe.

And for the most part, that truth set me free, free from fear and free to hope and trust God more.

Well some of the people in our life were having their own tough time with Bobby's condition, which prompted the following beautiful discourse.

Subject: To scream or not to scream…that is the question.

Dear Uncle Bobby:

I think of you often, but it's taken me a while to think through everything that's happening to you. When Tess and I visited you at home just after Christmas, you said you were trying to hang in there. I could hear the strain in your voice, and it scared me. At age 45 I still don't deal well with seeing loved ones suffer, but I should have stayed a while longer and let you know how much I admired the courage it must take to bear this burden every day like Sisyphus. I didn't stay, because I didn't know what to tell you—how to keep on trying or why to keep on trying.

You were always the strong, bright, confident one with an answer or a joke for almost every situation. And there was also your faith; the faith that brought your marriage and your family closer together and filled your lives with love. You don't deserve to have that faith and that love challenged with this disease; it makes me want to scream at somebody.

This would be cruel and unusual punishment if you were convicted of a heinous crime. But instead, you've made your life and the lives of those around you better…so I don't know who to be mad at or blame. Oddly enough, I learned to let go (most of the time) of that kind of anger from my parents…who knew?
You and I both know that I'm not likely to turn up as a Deacon in any parish anytime soon, but you should know that you and Aunt Joanne have at least given me faith in faith. Tess and I keep you in our thoughts and prayers. Sometimes I'd still rather yell at someone, but for now I'll just cherish family and friends a little more.

Love,
Jack & Tess

Subject: Re: To scream or not to scream…that is the question.
        You can scream all you want as long as it's in prayer. That's the answer.

Dear Jack & Tess

Thanks for the great letter.

There's no one to scream at or blame, suffering's a part of life. It's hard and I couldn't handle it without a strong belief in God. I am confirmed in how I've tried to live my life; I'm surrounded by love and faithfulness. God is very present and is carrying us through to victory—to life (preferably, here).

When I can focus on anything other than getting my next breath, I am aware of and thankful for the great life I've had: for my faith, my beautiful family and wonderful friends, the long years of good health and true happiness. I've loved and been loved a lot—life's too good to give up on.

Cherishing is good—do more of it and more often. And Jack, discover God's plan for your life and live it generously. He promises an "abundant life": life to the full, and he delivers more than can be anticipated.

We love you,
Uncle Bobby & Aunt Joanne

18

"Then Jesus said, "Did I not tell you that if you believed you would see the glory of God."

—John 11:40

14th mail

Subject: "The eternal God is your refuge, and underneath are the everlasting arms."
    Deuteronomy 33:27
Date: Monday, February 2, 2004 9:58 p.m.

Doesn't that sound comforting:"underneath are the everlasting arms?" Well let us tell you, they are more than comforting—they are more than enough—and they are carrying us close to His heart. We just got the news—Bob made it—He's on the Lung Transplant Waiting List!!! You prayed with us in earnest and now you can praise with us in joy and thanksgiving—Praise you God, Thank you Jesus for the powerful way you're working in our lives—for your everlasting love and faithfulness.

"This is the confidence we have in approaching God: that if we ask anything according to his will, He hears us. And if we know that he hears us—whatever we ask—we know that we have what we asked of him." 1 John 5:14-15 Alleluia!!!

We're on our way—Phase I Evaluation is over and we're now in Phase II Preparing/Waiting for Transplant. There are 4 Phases, (III Surgery and IV Post Transplant)—please continue to remain strong in praying in agreement with us—remembering that God's will is for Life and He is willing and able…to hear us—to perform a miracle for my honey—to keep him strong…to supply a new lung at the perfect time—Amen.

"I wait for you O Lord; you will answer O Lord my God." Psalm 38:15

We close with a heart of thanksgiving and praise,
Joanne and Bobby

P.S. Know that as you pray for us, we are praying for you and yours—that you each live in God's will for your life, that you are blessed with good health, peace, love and joy, and that all your needs are met.

Some responses to getting on the Lung Transplant Waiting List:

"Jo and Bob,
I just received the wonderful news. One day at a time, all things are possible—God bless,
Love you, Rene" (Florida)

"PRAISE THE LORD!!!!! Oh we're so happy. We love you guys so much. Blondie" (Florida)

"Oh what great news!!!!! Alleluia, alleluia, alleluia, Praise God! What a great Father!!! Our mass tomorrow and Tues. evening prayers will be pouring out in praise and joy and thanksgiving for this long awaited

news. Thanks for this gift of joy. Will print out your love letter and share with the gang.
Love you, Al & Marie"
(Florida)

This powerful and timely Word came from our Tennessee community through another prayer warrior, Val:
"Let go. My ways are not your ways. I will not be boxed in by your limitations. I am able to do immeasurably above and beyond all you can ask or think. I am the God of miracles and the doer of impossible things. You can do all things through me. I desire an open heart and willingness to break free. I desire obedience and actions based on faith.

My plan will not fail. Victory is the end of the matter. Let this truth set you free. Let my love shield you from the worries of this world. Let my desire for more of you ignite your desire for more of me. I love you with a love that is unfathomable in its magnitude yet is designed to reach you at the exact point of your unique and individual need. Perfect love casts out all fear. Fear not. Let go."

19

"The angels of the Lord are encamped around those who fear the Lord and they will deliver them."

—*Psalm 34:7*

Finally, the Transplant Team reviewed my case and I was put on the Transplant List January 30, 2004. Actually, there are three lists. Local, Regional and National. When a lung becomes available it's first offered locally. If there are no matches then it goes regionally and then nationally.

Once on the list, almost all the tests would have to be repeated every 3 to 6 months to ensure that I was still in relatively good condition. The first one coming up was the Six Minute Walk. I had already completed one and walked 1012 steps, and it was excruciating. Even with oxygen, recovery had taken what seemed like forever. We kept checking the oximeter, which measured my oxygen saturation and heart rate, hoping to see some signs of improvement there, even though they weren't apparent in my heaving chest.

We were up and down like a roller-coaster, relieved of one hurdle only long enough to catch our breath for the next one.

If I couldn't do 600 steps on this upcoming test, I would be taken off the list. That was a big worry of mine—Joanne's too. We both knew how weak I was and how little I could walk. I hadn't been able to do six consecutive minutes even at Rehab—I could only do two minutes at a time and have to sit, rest and wait to recover. But neither of us verbalized our worry. We knew the worst thing to lose at this point was hope; and we didn't want our words to be prophetic, and have our feet follow our tongue's hopeless words.

Tuesday, Feb. 17th, 2004

Bob has to do another six minute walk on Thursday (2/19 @ 11:30 a.m.). Joanne has asked for our prayers that he will have the strength to successfully complete the six minutes. We can do the "Breath Prayer" again…at 11:30 a.m. on Thursday. Bob's Breath Prayer is "Holy Spirit, walk with Bob and give him strength."
Let's storm the gates of heaven!!!!

Christ's peace,
Richie for Anne Marie

And from old friends in Queens, NY who shared with us our first real experience of Christian Community, through Marriage Encounter:

Dear Bob & Joanne,

We had dinner with Jack & Lorrie tonight and you were our absolute first thoughts. They told us they recently called and spoke to you briefly. You continue to be in all of our prayers and we do believe in His healing power. You will do the "six minutes" and our God will work his miracles in you and through you.

God Bless!
Love, Joan & Jerry

20

"I have fought the good fight, I have finished the race, I have kept the faith."

—2 Timothy 4:7

15th email

Subject: Six Minute Walk
Date: February 19, 2004   11:01 p.m.

Praise God, he did it! It was very hard—"the toughest thing I ever had to do"—but he couldn't miss with so many heartfelt prayers. 790 steps, each carried by prayer!

Have to share with you one of the readings we had this past week. "The cries of your sufferings have pierced even to the ears of God himself—My Father in Heaven, your Father in heaven. To hear, with God is to answer. For only a cry from the heart, a cry to Divine Power to help human weakness, a trusting cry, ever reaches the Ear Divine. Remember, trembling heart, that with God, to hear is to answer. Your prayers, and they have been many, are answered."

Psalm 77:14—"You are the God who performs miracles. You display your power among the peoples."

With love, thanks and praise,
Joanne and Bobby

◆   ◆   ◆

A lot of people were praying for me the day of the test, and every step I took I said the name of Jesus. Jesus…Jesus…Jesus…I knew I couldn't make it without him. I forced myself to continue. The oxygen I had wasn't satisfying my need. I wanted to give up, to stop, but I couldn't. It seemed to go on forever, then finally it was over. My lungs seemed to be bursting and I was gasping for air, I collapsed into the wheelchair. Joanne who watched each agonizing step, was crying tears of relief; I had traveled 790 steps and wouldn't be taken off the list. Thank you Jesus. Praise you God.

Also as mentioned before, the average waiting time on the Transplant List is 12 to 18 months. I knew I didn't have that kind of time and was afraid I wouldn't last until a lung became available. I told Joanne again that I was getting worse, I wanted her to be prepared, if that's possible. I was using higher and higher levels of oxygen and the slightest activity caused deep shortness of breath. It seemed to take forever to recover. There was always a little fear that that next breath wouldn't come.

◆   ◆   ◆

Through it all, we prayed our hearts out, praying in Jesus' name and reassuring ourselves that…anything you ask the Father in the name of Jesus, you will receive. We asked for a miracle and stood firmly rooted in His Word, believing His promises were true. And those dark times when we felt our faith faltering, we prayed "Lord we believe, help our unbelief."
How would we have been able to go on, without faith? We recognized and acknowledged it as the greatest survival asset we had. Thank you God for the priceless gift of faith, our pearl of great worth.

Some Six Minute Walk responses:

We received this treasure from our precious 5 year old granddaughter and it squeezed our hearts:

"DEAR GRAMMY AND POPPY I HOP POPPY FELS BETTER SOON AND I HOP I CAN SEE GRAMMY AND POPPY SOONN AND I PRADE FOR POPPY FOR THE HOL 6 MINIT WOK I LOVE YOU FROM JULIA WETZEL"

"Joanne & Bobby,
All we can say is "GOD BLESS YOU BOTH". Our hearts were heavy at 11:30. Now we are glad. "Prayer brings grace and grace enables us to accomplish the impossible."
Love you both,
Sal & Jennie" (Long Island, NY)

"We knew you were going to make it with HIS help!!! Thank you Jesus!!! So happy to hear the good news. Keep up the good work, we'll keep praying. Love, Hector and Cuqui.........big hug and kiss for you both!!" (Queens, NY)

Bob—
Showers of love are coming from your faith community here…We're so proud of the great efforts you are putting forth which encourages us, as well as amazes us. We are all in awe of your faith and courage during this difficult time. You are truly an inspiration and a living witness to faith in Jesus.

We'll all be jubilant on the day of your reward—a new lung(s). We confidently await that news and will stay the course with you. Run the race Bob and you will be rewarded. Your spirit is here and we continue to meet and pray for you daily.

With so much love, expectancy and faith,
Barbara & Joe (Florida)

Dear Dad,

Just a short note to share a thought I had while doing my reading for Pastoral Formation. This morning [while traveling to the City] John C and I were talking about the serious work load required to become a deacon. As I was reading tonight, this thought crossed my mind: What could they possibly teach me at the seminary that I haven't learned from watching you all these years? Keep up the good work!

I love you,
Mark

Dear Aunt Joanne & Uncle Bobby,

I was reading a book and couldn't concentrate on the words because thoughts of you were clouding my concentration. I often think about you, both so loving, both so vital, and both so filled with life-force that is undeniably the most powerful of all…true love—sweet, tender, gentle, abundant, generous love.

I wish I had the words to say that can enlighten or brighten your outlook. But I don't, I don't have those words. But, what I have to say to you is thank you and I love you; that you have always been my beacon of strength, and of love and good decisions. Aunt Joanne, you are an amazing woman. Because you are a woman I get where that comes from, sort of. But Uncle Bobby, you are beyond amazing because you are a man, who knew? Aunt Joanne, that's who knew.

You are both in my prayers because I pray all the time and you are always in my heart. You have always loved and accepted me, given me so much time when I had questions or doubts. But most of all what you gave me was the divine pleasure of watching the two of you love each other. My life is blessed by seeing you both so together in love.

You were always there for me and my family. You gave so much of your time and life to my mother and father when they needed you. You by definition are my "family". I wanted to thank you both and tell you that I admire you so much, and I am honored that you love me. I pray all the time for you Uncle Bobby, not sure what to pray for so it sort of goes in the "anything that is gonna' help him get through this okay" bin. And I pray for both of you that you are not in too much pain, that God soothes your broken hearts and quickly mends you back together again.

I love you,
Claire

21

"You are the God who performs miracles; you display your power among the peoples."

—*Psalm 77:14*

The last time Dr. Simonelli examined Bobby on February 5th, he was more solemn than usual and he said a number of times, "You need a lung"; Dr. Wilt too, (our wonderful Transplant Team Pulmonalogist) examining him after the Six Minute Walk February 19th, compassionately said the same, "You need a lung". (We later learned she passed that same concern on to Dr. Sonett—he needs a lung now.) Each time I thought, God's working on it. He'll get one in His time.

The exuberance we felt over Bobby's successful Six Minute Walk was short lived as his condition went from bad to worse in a matter of days. Crushing feelings of profound sadness filled me as I had to acknowledge that if he didn't get a lung and get it fast, he wasn't going to make it much longer. Bobby knew it too, and a couple of times, while he was thinking: "how nice it would be for me if I didn't wake up tomorrow", he said to me instead, "This is no way to live". But each morning upon awakening, he'd pray three short, heartfelt prayers: "Thanks Lord for waking me up; let me remember that nothings gonna happen today that you and I can't handle, and give me the grace to trust you more."

Slowly and spontaneously, little bits at a time, over those next days we shared the feelings we were experiencing with one another. I didn't want Bobby to be alone in this, and I wanted to be sure that he knew how much he was loved.

I remember one night in particular as we finished our usual prayers of praise and thanksgiving, I cried out to God with all the pain within me, telling him it was getting late and begging him to perform a miracle now. I asked him, "God what are we not doing that we should be doing—tell me what to do and we'll do it." His response was immediate and rang clearly in my head and heart: "Trust me more". It struck true and reassuringly. I told Bobby what God said, and we agreed to stretch ourselves even more—with God's help, we could stretch and reach and touch the hem of his garment. Nothing was impossible, nothing too hard for God.

By Monday, February 23ʳᵈ most of my hope was gone and I felt helpless, empty and scared. I knew God had not abandoned us, and I was trusting him with all my might, but I was so fearful that although I did believe his will is for Life, it appeared that his will for Bobby just might be life in heaven. And I couldn't bear the thought of being without him. We had been together since I was fifteen years old, fifty one years, I wasn't even sure I'd be me without him. I was losing the best part of myself.

Over the next few days, we talked occasionally about that and of how good God had always been to us, how blessed we were in our love and life, our children and friends all these years. How if we could do it all over, we'd make the same choices. I told him how much I'd miss him, and he told me he wasn't afraid but that he hated to cause me pain.

Then came Thursday night, an exceptionally bad one, Bobby couldn't get any rest at all and we ended up spending the night in the den, getting moments here and there of fitful sleep. Friday was supposed to be an exercise day at Helen Hayes Hospital, and for the first time, Bobby said, "I can't go" and, of course, I knew that.

We moved to the living room where it was brighter and more spacious and, except for moving a small fan around the room and trying one pillow after another in an attempt to get him somewhat comfortable, we spent a quiet, prayerful day together. We were very much together, and with no need for words. That night, however, as part of our prayers, we thanked God for His faithfulness, for never abandoning us, for the miracle of knowing that whether Bobby was here or in heaven, God would take care of him and me. We'd both be fine and continue to be where we always had been, in the palm of God's hands.

I surrendered us both to God's will that night, not my perception of it, but His will whatever it was. I told Bobby he didn't have to stay here for me, but that while things were looking very grim, I just didn't believe that God was taking him to heaven now—"deep within me I still believe we're going to get our miracle." He said, "that's good honey, you believe for both of us." We hugged, kissed goodnight and fell into a peaceful sleep.

Then the phone was ringing—it was the middle of the night. Oh no, it's only 2:15 and now Bobby's awake. "Hello. Is Robert Wetzel there? [Yes] This is Columbia Presbyterian Hospital [was someone playing a cruel joke? No, no, but they said 12—18 months, it's not even a month]—Dr. Sonett asked me to call, we have a possible lung match…How soon can you get here?…Can you get someone to drive you…drive carefully…" Even on the phone, I could hardly contain my joy. Oh my God, my God, my great and mighty God. Thank you God, Father, Son and Holy Spirit—you are all powerful, all merciful, true to your promises. We prayed in Jesus' name—ask anything in His name and you will receive it—here it is, our miracle! What a mighty God we serve. Oh my God, I am overwhelmed by the depths of your love and mercy. Thank you Jesus, thank you Jesus. I only stopped praising God long enough to hug and kiss my sweetheart and tell him and my daughter-in-law, Cathy, who came up to see who was on the phone, that we had a lung match and had to get to the hospital as fast and safely as we could.

We laughed and cried and got ready to go. While I was still on the phone, Bobby realized what the call was about and said, "He's giving me my shot." He repeated that several times on the drive down. We were fearless—fear is not of God, and God was definitely with us—we held hands and I praised God in prayer and song for all of us. To Him is all glory now and for-ever—and all the way down the Palisades Parkway to the Transplant floor of Presbyterian Hospital.

"To the drowning man the rescuer comes—so you will recognize who he is…" Oh we had no doubt Who was rescuing us—He had shown us His face all along—had revealed His plan in His promises, and for the most part, we believed and acknowledged Him and always persevered in prayer. All of us together, and all of us have a share in this wonderful miracle, this sign of God with us.

From the very moment I understood what the call was, I knew with cer-tainty that the lung would be a match and Bobby would survive the opera-tion. A four hour operation turned into seven, then eight hours and I never wavered; our whole family never wavered. We stood firm in God's promises. We prayed for new lungs and long life and from the beginning God's response through his Word always spoke life to our hearts. To us this "eleventh hour" lung match and surgery were confirmation that God is true to His Word.

We prayed for a miracle, and we got one!

> *"I will not die but live and proclaim the good works of the Lord."*
> —Psalm 118:17

EPILOGUE

"My soul will boast in the Lord; let the afflicted hear and rejoice. Glorify the Lord with me; let us exalt His name forever."

—*Psalm 34:2-3*

God had planned every detail brilliantly. At no point had I said to our children, "this is it, you'd better come up." They had been there all along, and each in his and her own way had done all they could and said all they wanted to say. They also knew their father's condition, and were trusting God for a miracle. But that night of nights, with no orchestration from me, or each other, a master plan unfolded.

Laurie and Anthony who live in Tennessee were up visiting us for a few days, (it would have been awful if they were a thousand miles away)—she already was dreading leaving. That morning, they brought the baby to see Anthony's sister in New Jersey, which allowed them to come immediately to the hospital, leaving the baby in his aunt's loving care. Chris and Cathy too, spent that night with us at the spur of the moment and without their five year old, Julia—they never did that. Julia was happily with her little cousin and Cathy's sister. And as if that weren't enough, it was the weekend, and no one had to be concerned about jobs.

It would have taken me forever to get Bobby and all the oxygen tanks down the stairs and into the car; Chris, however, with very little help from Cathy and me, was able to get him down in the wheelchair. Cathy called Mark and Kathy, Scott, Laurie and Anthony as I dressed Bobby and myself, and all eight of us were able to be at the hospital, waiting, praying, standing strong in the Lord together, (later joined and further uplifted by brother Ed and sister-in-law Audrey and niece, Kathleen and her husband, Tom.)

We were held up high the whole time by the continuing prayers of all our "churches" in New York, Florida, Tennessee, North Carolina, New Jersey, Connecticut and Georgia, all of whom we didn't hesitate calling from 5 to 6 in the morning when Bobby was wheeled into surgery, to let them know their prayers were answered, our miracle was in progress.

All of whom squealed with delight, words of praise to the Lord and encouragement and promises of continued prayers for us.

And the good news and updates continues to spread far and wide…

"We just received a phone call from Bernadette. Bob is in surgery (since 5:30 a.m.)—he got his lung. Prayers are needed now, maybe more than ever! Please pray that he will remain strong throughout the surgery and that he will not reject the lung. Also pray for the family of the donor, this is a very difficult time for them. Love ~~ AM" (Rockland, NY)

16th email
Saturday, February 28, 2004

BOB GOT HIS LUNG!

FOR HE HAS DONE GREAT THINGS—ALLELUIA!!!

COME ON AND BLESS THE LORD, OH MY SOUL, AND ALL
THAT IS WITHIN ME, BLESS HIS HOLY NAME!!…
We just got in from the hospital—he's looking good. We'll go back tomor-
row.
We feel your love and prayers—keep 'em coming!!

Laurie (on behalf of Joanne)

BOB GOT HIS LUNG!

If you think you have never seen or heard of a miracle before you can say you have now. Against all the earthly odds this operations should never have happened. He was too old for the transplant list, his lungs were in bad shape, he got on the list too late, his blood type was rare and he was losing his strength. You prayed hard and your prayers were answered. God strengthened his body and he made it through all the tests, went through the interview and was put on the list. He walked 1012 steps the first six minute walk and 790 the second walk and your prayers were with him every step. When the doctors operated on Bob they said that they wouldn't have performed the surgery if they would have know how bad a condition he was in…yet he passed every test. A 4 hour operation took 9 hours and he had the strength to endure…because of your prayers.

Continue to pray for a speedy and full recovery for our Brother Bob and strength for Joanne and the Wetzel family.

Your brother in Christ,
Richie (Rockland, NY)

WOW, God is truly Great. Wow from Hawaii @ 5:26 am. Love you all, miss you all and we are truly feeling you all with us at this time thru prayer…
Ed & Nancy (Rockand, NY, vacationing in Hawaii)

How Great Is Our God!!!! AMEN!!!! The power of prayer from our beautiful Christian Community has stormed the gates!!!! Keep saying those prayers for the Wetzel Family and give praise to the God who has saved us!!!
xoxo
Josine & John (Rockland, NY)

"There are two ways to live…..One…as if nothing were a miracle…The other as if everything were a miracle…" Each day, each breath, a miracle! Your faith and this miracle has made a lasting impression on our hearts and on our faith…We are forever thankful to our God—for you and your lessons on trust and hope and acceptance. Our God reigns—forever and ever!
Paul & Bernadette (Rockland, NY)

…you're all in my prayers 24-7, Bobby especially. Many people here are praying and lifting him up to the Lord. We all remain steadfast in our prayers that all is going well….may our heavenly Father keep you all safe and secure in the palm of His hand.
I love you very much,
Lois (Connecticut)

How marvelous, astonishing, wonderful!!! Not enough descriptive words to proclaim the miracle before our eyes….Sharing your miracle has brought hope to so many and we will never know all the lives you

touched with all you have gone through and allowed yourselves to share and let in to be a part of this love story. The rosary group at St. Mark's beyond delighted and they were beaming when I shared your news. We love you guys and praise our sweet Jesus…
Thanks for the joy of today,
Al & Marie (Florida)

Whoever gets this in time can say a breath prayer for Bob at 8:00 a.m. when they take him off the ventilator and he takes his first breath with his new lung. HOLY SPIRIT, SURROUND BOB WITH YOUR HEALING LIGHT AND GIVE HIM STRENGTH.
Have a good day,
AnneMarie (Rockland, NY)

17th email
Wednesday, March 3, 2004
Praise the Lord, Oh my Soul!

Just a quick note from Laurie—Mom is at the hospital—Dad is off the ventilator as of this morning! He's doing well, and the nurse even had him say hello to mom on the phone! His voice was very low, so she didn't hear him, but I'm sure she's there now rejoicing with her Sweetheart!

They may move him to a lesser ICU tomorrow. Keep the prayers coming—Our Lord hears them and is happy to give us the desires of our hearts!

Good Morning and Good news
…Bob is totally off the ventilator and he's doing great…..Just give him time to get up to speed and he'll be telling you about the glory of the Lord…Hallelujah and Amen. God is good all the time.

Stay alert, stay on guard, keep praying…keeping this family covered in prayer is something we can all do..
Love to you all,
Diana (Tennessee)

My heart is happy, there's a great smile on my face and praise on my lips. What wonderful, but not unexpected news. Love you both and will continue to keep you in prayer.
Carole (New Jersey)

What a blessing to be a part of one of God's miracles. We were blessed to share in your journey.
We love you guys!
Mike & Dottie (North Carolina)

Thank you Jesus for Bobby, and thank you Bobby for allowing us all to believe so much more through your pain and suffering. Your journey through the valley has led all of us to the mountain top. Praise God always and forever—we sing His praises.
With so much love,
Barbara & Joe (Florida)

Praise God and Thank you Jesus! You and Joanne are in our hearts and prayers every day….You are so much a part of us as family and friend, how good God is.
Thank God for the power of prayer…what a wonderful miracle we have all seen!….
With the joy & peace of our Lord,
Johnny & Dolores (Florida)

Dear Bobby (Miracle Man) We don't have the right words to express our joy for the great work God has done for you. We always said we believe in miracles, but now that we have experienced yours, we know we believe!

Your brother & sister in Christ,

Joe & Mary (Florida)

Love you!—love you!—love you!

We have witnessed several miracles through you—you/we are truly blessed.....We are still getting up at 7:15 a.m. every day for Mass for both of you (that's a miracle in itself). We're always praying for you. Because of your [courage and faith] I never lost faith in you and God. I knew he'd see you through it all.

Love you,

Catherine and Joe (Florida)

You are living proof of the power of prayer…a miracle!

God Bless you,

Virginia & Andy (From Florida)

18th email

Thursday, March 11, 2004

This is the day the Lord has Made!

You've shared our sorrow and halved it, now share our joy and double it!

Bobby is oxygen free and Baby Emily is a reality [we received word in the hospital that the grandchild we'd been waiting for was finally cleared to be picked up in China]. All in today's joy!!!

Look at what prayer has wrought—abundant blessings on the Wetzel family. "Pressed down and running over…"—we are overwhelmed by his and your love and faithfulness…

With a heart overflowing with thanksgiving—we stand in awe and praise you O Lord!!!

P.S. Keep those prayers coming—we love these blessings!!!!! Bobby is going up to Rehab tomorrow. What a day!!!!

What a beautiful tribute you, Bob and your family are to our faith! As always, you continue to inspire me to keep going and keep praying ~ even when things seem to be desperate. I am thinking of all of you always! God bless ~
Karen (Rockland, NY)

19th email
Thursday, March 25, 2004

"You are the God who performs miracles; You display your power among the peoples." Psalm 77:14

Well he's not home yet but he's on his way! Per Bobby's wonderful doctors, he's been experiencing some "bumps in the road"—they told me not to worry and told him: "you're like an old car, just need finer tuneups".

While we're disappointed that this hasn't been going in a straight line and Bobby didn't come home today, we know God has him covered and, just as he supplied him with a lung at the perfect time, he'll bring him home at the perfect time.

We continue to rely on your positive prayers—they brought us amazing miracles and they'll bring him to full recovery. Like Dr. Simonelli (our doctor who asked the Team to make an exception for Bobby) said when he saw us after the surgery—"you prayed for a miracle and you got one!"

We also continue to give all glory and praise to our Faithful, Awesome, Loving God.

The prayer/song playing constantly within us is one from our old Howard Beach Prayer Meeting—I wish you all knew it, it fills you up and brings you right into the Throne room—COME ON AND BLESS THE LORD, O MY SOUL, AND ALL THAT IS WITHIN ME, BLESS HIS HOLY NAME—FOR HE HAS DONE GREAT THINGS—ALLELUIA, HE HAS DONE GREAT THINGS, ALLELUIA, HE HAS DONE GREAT THINGS—BLESS HIS HOLY NAME!!!

Love you all,
Joanne and Bobby

It is so good to hear from you and feel connected. I, too, love the Psalms. Ps. 139 v. 14 "I will praise thee, for I am fearfully and wonderfully made: marvelous are thy works; and that my soul knoweth right well" makes me think of Bobby being wonderfully made with his new lung given to him by Our Lord. I am so happy for you both and pray that God give you many years together to enjoy and savor the gift. You have been His "good servants" and He has blessed you. I know that you give Him all the glory. May Bobby continue to heal and get stronger every day.
Love you both,
Carole (N.J.)

MIRACLES—WHY FOR SOME, NOT ALL?

If you're going to pray for a miracle, ask others to pray for it with you, or simply speak of believing in miracles, you better be prepared to address the age old question that will arise—WHY? Why do some receive miracles and others do not?

Hi Aunt Joanne & Uncle Bobby,

My God you all look so beautiful, and happy and HEALTHY! [hospital email pictures]
God has blessed you! And I know will continue to do so.

Aunt Jo, you must call my brother and get his email, or I will get it for you. He needs to hear your messages and proof of God answering all of our prayers for you and your family and my uncle.

I HAVE A QUESTION.
Why is it that I believe that he answers others prayers, and I really do believe that, I see it, I get it…but not so sure that he answers mine?

Please don't say because I don't go to church…or don't have faith…I believe in his miracles. Did what happened to Jamie happen or better yet not end in a miracle, because we didn't pray enough? I don't know, maybe so. I hope not though. I prayed every minute. Maybe that's why I believe he answers some but not all people's prayers.

> [When Claire was 11 years old her brother Jamie, 17, was in a tragic car accident causing him to suffer severe brain damage and exist five years in a comatose state before dying.]

He knocks people off horses and allows Jesus to redeem a prostitute. Do I need to hit bottom I hope not. I think the way I feel tonight is as low a bottom as I really can go right now.

As I write this letter I think, OK maybe I should go to church, but I gotta tell you, it just doesn't do it for me. Practice my faith. Like exercise. You don't see results right away but…it works if you work it..ick!

I love you. I realize I'm feeling a little lost tonight. Maybe that's a good place to start. It took me long enough to get here, or see I am here. I always knew I was a late bloomer!

I'm sorry that I just turned your totally happy sharing into something about me. But it just sort of spilled out. The other thing is I am really truly happy for anyone's prayers that are answered. It makes me believe even more. I don't think there's a limit on "answered prayers" in that area, I definitely believe in abundance.

Love you,
Your niece that holds you in such a special place in my heart, you have no idea.

Dear Claire,

"…Oh my gosh, I just this minute realized it's your birthday!!! I've spent all day thinking of you…and only now did it pop into my head out of nowhere. Now how can I get back to such a serious topic when it's your birthday?
Happy Birthday Claire Ann—this year has taken it's toll on me, yours is a birthday I never forget!

Well for one thing—it's a great time for new beginnings.

Gotta get back to your questions—this is a tough one and I could go on and on (I'll try not to). Your email wrenched my heart. Wish I had THE answers; I don't, but I'll try to give you what I have. I, like most, have the same questions you asked. WHY? Why Uncle Bobby and not the lung donor? Why not Aunt Blondie's friend, Vickie—we were praying for her at the same time? Why not all the others—younger, healthier, mothers and fathers of small children—children, other people's loved ones? Jamie???

You asked what happened to Jamie? What happened happened because they were speeding and lost control of the car; there usually are consequences to pay for our actions/decisions/choices (fortunately most times not life and death ones). And oh we certainly did pray enough—we prayed every waking moment from the depths of our hearts (I believe that's important—heartfelt prayers). Did we have enough people praying? I don't know, I think so. Did we expect a miracle? I'm not sure. Does any of that matter? I'm not so sure of that either.

Is there a correct prayer formula for miracles? I think not—I believe less depends on us and more on God, but we're absolutely in it together. Something is required of us—perhaps faith, prayer and actions that radiate them. Not entirely sure just what—certainly faith, (which, by the way, you do have) and an expectant faith helps—like the bible story of the woman suffering with hemorrhages; she dragged herself through the crowds believing that if she could just touch the hem of his garment, she'd be healed. We have to be willing to do our part: to stretch ourselves to reach him, believing he'll respond. And of course he always does—but not always in the way we hoped .

I believe that much of life and God is mystery. His ways aren't our ways; he's operating on a higher plain with a greater purpose; beyond my understanding. And that's okay 'cause I trust him. He's good and is working to good all the time.

Now church. Church isn't the end all and the be all, (I often enjoy a good prayer meeting or retreat more myself) but it could help, it could lead to something more. Besides, your soul's probably suffering from malnutrition. It needs its "daily bread" (or weekly) and a good helping of the Word to ponder and grow on. (Thy word is a lamp unto my feet and a light unto my path.)

He knocked Paul off his horse and Paul picked himself up and turned from persecuting Christians to being a great Apostle, bringing the Good News to the then-known world. As for the prostitute, she knelt at his feet, got up and turned her life around as well.

Do you need to hit bottom? Not for God you don't, maybe for yourself. I don't have the answer, you have to turn to God not me. He has your answers, and you have to be willing to "walk the walk" in obedience to his Word. Ask, listen, wait for his response, (perhaps look in the bible for guidance and direction) and then OBEY it. I'm not judging you Claire, believe me, I know you're good and wonderful and love you with all my heart, but obedience isn't one of your strong points...(I can't "throw the first stone" 'cause it hasn't been one of mine either). "God answers the prayers of righteous men [and women]". Righteous are those in good standing with the Lord, they've placed themselves under his authority, and believe and obey him…(Warned you I could go on and on.)

Gonna' close now with Jeremiah 29 vs. 11-13. "For I know the plans I have for you, declares the Lord, "plans to prosper you and not to harm you, plans to give you hope and a future. Then you will call upon me and come and pray to me, and I will listen to you. You will seek me and find me when you seek me with all your heart."

I know Claire that birthday reflections can be brutal…try to reach out and fill the gaps with Jesus—he can make the difference…

Love you just as you are,
Aunt Joanne

20th email
Thursday, April 1, 2004
He's Home at last!

Be it ever so humble—emotional—overwhelming—WONDER-FUL—there's no place like home! Just wanted to let you know BOBBY'S HOME—and home never looked or felt so good.

He still has a long, long way to go—we're trusting God and are filled with confidence that he is continuing the wonderful work he began. We wish we could convey to you how blessed and loved we feel by your untiring prayers and support as well. Sorry we can't let you "off the hook" just yet, in fact this phase of the transplant, Post Transplant, lasts forever! Just approach it as we are, one day at a time and keep your eyes on Jesus and our names on your Prayer List, as yours are on ours—and in our hearts, always. Thank you all so, so much.

We love you,
Joanne and Bobby

We continue to see God's hand on us as our story goes on. But for now we close, urging you to stand firm in the scriptures. You have to know the promises of God to stand strong in them, to claim them, and to live in the will of God, wherein lies inner peace and true joy.

978-0-595-36184-7
0-595-36184-6

Printed in the United States
35365LVS00006B/121-180